TOMBSTONES

OF

YOUR ANCESTORS

By Louis S. Schafer

IN LOVING MEMORY
of
THOMAS F. JONES
Born
Nov'r 4, 1889
Died
May 23, 1927

May he rest in peace

HERITAGE BOOKS, INC.

Published 1991 By

HERITAGE BOOKS, INC.
1540-E Pointer Ridge Place
Bowie, MD 20716
(301) 390-7709

ISBN 1-55613-436-3

A Complete Catalog Listing Hundreds of Titles on
History, Genealogy & Americana
Free on Request

This project is warmly dedicated to the memory of my mother-in-law, Betty Ilene Brandt, who helped me realize that death is simply an extension of life, and to my loving wife, Brenda Sue, whose bravery taught me the true meaning of courage.

Contents

Preface

This book is intended to be an introduction to the hobby of locating, deciphering, and collecting gravestone inscriptions and carvings. It has been written, for the most part, as a guide for three types of people: (1) those who are conducting extensive research into family genealogy and history; (2) those who are simply intrigued by early American heritage, and (3) those who are in the process of assembling an extensive collection of curious tombstone poetry and sculpture.

Even though numerous people have often thought about gathering a collection of early American epitaphs and tombstone imagery, they may never begin such an enriching hobby simply because they do not know where or how to start. Presently, there is very little written material available for the amateur collector. Furthermore, there are few experts who can advise you on the pursuit of this fascinating pastime. Therefore, I hope that this book will also be used by librarians and genealogical experts who might be willing to put beginning collectors on the right track.

A word of advice to those epitaph hobbyists researching their family heritage: don't get your hopes up too high. For the vast majority of men, women, and children who have ever lived and died, there is, in many instances, a gravesite where he or she is buried. Still, the researcher may run into a few obstacles along the way: a particular grave may not be clearly marked, there may be difficulty in locating the specific burial site, or the cemetery itself may have been neglected to the point of being unrecognizable, or destroyed by progress.

Despite the strong likelihood, however, that a specific relative's grave cannot be located, other epitaphs from the same region in which they were born, lived, worked, and died will surely hint at the history of the times. After all, establishing a richer historical perspective is what truly concerns any avid epitaph collector.

Please keep in mind that, if you plan on following the detailed procedures outlined in this book, some communities have placed stringent restrictions upon people who visit their aging burial grounds. In fact, in one town that I passed through in southern Vermont, it was even illegal to *walk* through the cemetery, let alone read, decipher, transcribe, photograph, rub, trace, or make a mold of the tombstones. In many areas of the country, total restriction is the only way to protect our national heritage from possible abuse and destruction. Therefore, it is essential that you take the time to secure permission from the proper authorities before pursuing your chosen aspect of epitaph and tombstone sculpture collecting.

Chapter 1

Why Collect Epitaphs and Tombstone Sculpture

Sacred to the Memory
of Amasa Brainard, Jr.
Son of Lieut. Amasa & Mrs.
Jedidiah Brainard
who receiv'd a Mortal wound on his head
by the falling of a weight from the Bell
on Sunday, ye 22nd of Apl., 1798,
as he was about enter the Church to
attend on divine worship.

The number of enthusiasts pursuing the fascinating hobby of collecting early American epitaphs and tombstone artwork has been literally skyrocketing in the last few years. On any given day of the week, you may see ordinary citizens of all ages casually browsing through any one of a thousand burial grounds and cemeteries scattered all across America: gray-haired retirees laying flowers over the graves of their departed spouses; small groups of school children conducting intense scavenger hunts; as well as health-conscious individuals jogging leisurely along a graveyard's peaceful pathways. An out-of-the-way cemetery's uses are quite literally limitless.

In addition, there are those of us who simply find intrinsic beauty in a burial site's chiselled artwork and literature. Often you will spot us hard at work, reading, transcribing, tracing, photographing, rubbing, tin-foiling, and making intricate molds of headstones that are centuries old. From time to time, collectors such as myself are often momentarily interrupted by curious and somewhat perplexed onlookers who are intrigued by these unusual activities. And, by far, the predominant question that tombstone collectors and historical researchers are asked seems to be: "Why are you doing what you are doing?"

"Why, indeed!" I have often answered, just short of exasperation. Still, I understand that probing inquiries into the unusual activities of collectors are, quite frankly, well-founded. After all, such hobbies may seem, at least on the surface, to be a waste of time to the logical minds of those who have never enjoyed a quiet, sunny, summer afternoon browsing through a local cemetery. Indeed, a great deal of time and effort is required for those involved in the hobby of collecting epitaphs and headstone sculpture, and time today is an extremely scarce commodity.

Scores of people throughout America believe that burial sites should be reserved for grieving family members and friends, and that they should not be invaded by hobbyists. Besides, the mere thought of wandering through a cemetery sends shivers of revulsion up the spines of many people, who might view such pastimes as being distasteful, or even morbid. Still others feel that the overabundance of cemeteries and graveyards are an intrusive eyesore, and that they should be handed over to developers, who may be able to use the surplus acreage for other more meaningful purposes. To them, it seems somewhat ludicrous to have a special place set aside for the deceased. Perhaps the citizens of Worcester, Massachusetts, felt the same way in 1853, when they decided to lay the stones of their cemetery face down. Today, the grave markers of more than 300 early settlers are lost from sight in this, the "hidden graveyard."

There are many others, however, including historians, preservationists, and hobbyists, who would adamantly disagree with such outdated and narrow-minded points of view. To them, ignoring death and burial means to ignore a very natural part of life. And if we should allow graveyards, like other archeological remnants, to become extinct, we are renouncing an irreplacable portion of our national history. After all, we must begin to appreciate the true value of these early American stone carvings before it is too late. Without a doubt, they make up a vast, untapped collection of early artwork and history that continues to survive today.

In reality, nowhere is the ever-changing nature of human life more vividly evident than in a quaint, rural cemetery, situated on a quiet hillside. Therein one can find early stones that are true archeological artifacts; yet unlike most other pieces of the past, they have not been excavated or extricated from their natural settings. In fact, grave markers have often remained in the same location in which they were originally positioned for hundreds of years. Obviously, much can be learned from them about our ancestral lineage and historical tide.

As time passes, however, American heritage is becoming victimized by neglect. More often than not, these somber grave-yards lie decaying and forgotten, submerged in a veritable sea of mystery. There are literally hundreds of such burial places scattered throughout the countryside. Frequently, few descendants of those whose remains are laid to rest beneath its hallowed ground live nearby. And in some instances the entire makeup of a region's population has changed over the years, with old families gradually dying off or moving away.

When such a transition does indeed occur, the graves that are left behind receive an inadequate amount of care. In time, brush and brambles grow so thick that not a single headstone can be seen. Eventually the markers topple over and sink passively beneath the ground. The digestive earth soon swallows them whole, as they become mere foundations for grass, weeds, dead leaves, and fallen limbs. Nature is unrelenting and if left unchecked, she will inevitably take control of all that remains unguarded.

Even when these historical markers continue to gallantly hold their erect posture, annual bouts with inclement weather may deteriorate and erode their intricately carved faces. Often, delamination occurs, as the layers of stone slowly separate and split apart along natural bedding planes. Furthermore, exfoliation and flaking, which are best described as the peeling and scaling of gravestone surfaces, may be brought about by both the constantly changing seasons and man-made pollution.

When aging monuments do somehow manage to survive the constant onslaught of rain, humidity, sun, snow, freezing temperatures, and human assault, they may be attacked from below the surface. Ever so slowly, rising dampness from the earth pushes moisture into the porous stone, much like water soaking into a sponge. This capillary-like action of water moving into rock brings with it soluble salts from the earth. And when this abrasive salt solution begins to crystallize within the open pores, it leaves behind a white, efflorescent film on the stone's surface. This encrustation will inevitably promote rotting from the inside out, eventually breaking away noticeable chunks. This process, known as spalling, will cause irreversible damage to the stone's surface.

The destruction of these national treasures, however, is not always brought about by natural forces; for there are virtually hundreds of ways that headstones may be damaged. At times, uncaring people have been known to degrade cemeteries and vandalize markers. For example, over the remains of John Holyoke, who was buried in a small Newton, Massachusetts, graveyard in 1775, researchers will find a severely pock-marked head-

3

stone. It is quite obvious that devious persons used his priceless marker for target practice. Similar criminal and unethical activities will undoubtedly continue to occur in graveyards that do not have some sort of preventative measures in force.

Sometimes, unintentional damage is caused by those very people who are put in charge of caring for cemeteries. Commercial herbicides have been known to permanently scar a stone; markers are sometimes moved and accidentally dropped, all in a futile desire to straighten out-of-line rows; and chemical cleaners tend to deface stone markers when used improperly. Perhaps the greatest threat to historic gravestones comes from modern-day landscaping techniques. Indeed, gasoline-powered lawn mowers have been the unwitting agents in a great many assaults, for they tend to hurl debris that can nick, scratch, gouge, scar, and even break through a marker's protective outer layers.

On other occasions, grave markers are moved by well-meaning--yet unthinking--cemetery caretakers, who believe that relocating forgotten stones will somehow lead to their preservation. Instead of being stored in a safe place, however, they are often simply leaned up against stone walls or trees. These old markers are then susceptible to being snatched up and carried away by thieves, only to be used as part of a foundation, a doorstep, or a conversation piece. Recently, a neighbor of mine decided to cut down an overgrowth of brush in an adjacent empty lot near his home. What do you suppose he accidentally struck with his hand-held sickle, but a stolen grave marker that dated back in time more than 150 years!

Finally, in some instances, wandering herds of deer, elk, moose, or even cows and sheep have been known to enter an ancient graveyard to graze upon the luscious grasses, shrubs, and sapling trees that often grow there. While there, they will scratch themselves or leave their mark by rubbing up against old stones. In the process one or two markers will be knocked over and trampled into the soft ground as the wayward herd moves on.

Hence, the burial spots of prominent members of American history can be lost forever due to natural events, deliberate acts, or chance and circumstance. One prime example of this occurred in Exeter, New Hampshire many years ago when the delicate roots of my own family tree were pulled up by unidentified forces. It was there, during the mid-1600's, that my great-great-great-great-great-great-great-great grandfather, John Sinkler, came to live.

In an effort to rescue this long-lost relative from his obscure place in history, I set out to research his heritage and his life. I found that he was only the second known person of this name to land on American soil, and was a descendant of one of the oldest, strongest, and most renowned families in all of Great Britain. His lineage travelled back in time through the medieval era of France; past the ancient castles of St. Clere and St. Lo; and across the fertile valleys surrounding the historic River Epte.

His name appeared time and time again in volumes recording Exeter's earliest affairs. There, he left behind significant clues to his existence: deeds for scores of acres purchased throughout the region; court records of a boundary dispute over that land with neighbors; birth records showing that he had fathered two sons and three daughters; and a detailed will dividing up his estate. After learning about Sinkler's life through these records, I then wished to conclude my research by studying his death.

Records show that John Sinkler submitted his final will and testament to the Probate Court on September 14, 1700. Sadly, however, the particulars of his death and burial were never recorded for the sake of posterity. Even more discouraging was the fact that no stone remains marking his gravesite, though it was written in township records that he was buried on the "north western slope of meeting house hill." Thus the chapter outlining the life of my ancestor John Sinkler--one of the earliest settlers in the New Hampshire region--remains incomplete. It is a great loss for both history and my family tree.

Such occurrences are not peculiar to my family heritage, for they have happened repeatedly in hundreds of other family trees which put down roots in thousands of communities throughout America. And the sad ending to such a story is also often repeated. Years later, there arrives an inquisitive ancestor, digging for any inscribed record which a headstone might exhibit. If he is extremely lucky, the researcher will indeed locate the ancient marker, and will record what it has to offer. Thus, he has saved a piece of heritage for future generations.

However, more often than not, good fortune is not with him in his search, for fate has destroyed the ancestor's headstone long ago. Epitaphs, like the lives of those who compose them and take the time to read them, are only temporary. Therefore it is essential that we act before it is too late, in order to preserve what remains of their vast wisdom and heritage. Whether it is for the purpose of gaining a bit of insight concerning a long-lost relative or to establish a more accurate portrait of American history, perusing tombstone literature can be an interesting and rewarding pastime.

A few years ago, during a summer vacation along the eastern seaboard, I spent some time visiting the New York metropolitan area. While there, I opted to visit a number of local cemeteries, in order to gain a truer sense of the region's history. In St. An-

5

drews churchyard, located in Staten Island, New York, I found an amusing epitaph dedicated to John Young, who died in 1836:

> Those that knew him best deplored him most.

More recently, while traveling through the mountains of Colorado, I made a point to browse through a number of local burial grounds. Carved on a large boulder near Mount Pisgah Cemetery in Cripple Creek, I discovered the following brief, yet telling, words:

> He Called
> Bill Smith
> A Liar.

During your search, you may find that generations past used a variety of materials to mark the burial spots of their dead. Normally, they incorporated what was most abundant in the vicinity, much of which has proved to be an enduring tribute.

Study the stones carefully. Notice that, as decades went by, the advancement of American culture led us to use such lasting commodities as sandstone, limestone, quartzite, slate, and marble on which to fashion epitaphs and artwork. This early interest in particular materials can reveal a good deal about the times: personal taste, specific stone carvers, trade routes, and commercial patterns.

Near Bennington, Vermont, for example, it seems quite obvious that the township's residents long preferred the polished look of marble from a nearby quarry to mark the burial sites of their deceased. Much further west, however, in regions like the Ohio Valley--where overland trade routes were extremely difficult to follow for hundreds of years--a wide variety of less durable field stones and local materials was used instead.

Epitaphs can reveal a good deal of pertinent information about a particular person. Such inscriptions are often the only surviving record concerning an individual's death. Many, in fact, are particularly detailed in the portrait they attempt to put forth. In the Old South Cemetery, located in Montague, Massachusetts, is an epitaph that graphically describes the demise of Elijah Bardwell, who died in 1786:

> In Memory of Mr. Elijah Bardwell
> who died....in ye 27th year of
> his Age having but a few days
> surviv'd ye fatal night when he
> was flung from his Horse & drawn

by ye Stirrup 26 rods along ye
path as appear'd by ye place where
his hat was found & where he had
Spent ye whole following severe cold
night treading ye Snow in a Small Circle

The upper portion of this monument is in the shape of a clock, which illustrates the once common belief that a clock would stop precisely at the moment of death.

Epitaphs can reveal much more than mere personal statistics concerning the life and death of the deceased. For example, they may offer a bit of insight into social attitudes, cultural happenings, and regional trends; hint at personal tragedy, catastrophic disasters, and outbreaks of early-day disease; or provide information concerning prejudice, discrimination, and personal relationships.

Some of the most revealing occurrences in America's past can be found in the words etched on tombstones. An unmistakably patriotic action, for example, might well have been forgotten to the annals of history if it weren't for the tombstone of Rebecca Jones, who was buried in Pleasant Grove Cemetery, near Raleigh, North Carolina:

Devoted Christian mother who whipped
Sherman's bummers with scalding water
while trying to take her dinner pot
which contained a ham bone being
cooked for her soldier boys.

Personal feelings which may be shared by the majority of a particular community's townsfolk can often be found etched into a single man's headstone. Sometimes, the words are both prophetic and moral, almost as a warning to future generations. Ezekiel Polk, grandfather of President James K. Polk, was not one to refrain from doling out criticism, and many believe that he spoke for a great many local citizens. Evidence of rigid prejudices against the "inevitable" joining of church and state are forever carved into his tombstone, which stands in Polk Cemetery, Bolivar, Tennessee:

Here lies the dust of old E. P.
One instance of mortality;
Pennsylvania born. Car'lina bred.
In Tennessee died on his bed.
His youthful days he spent in pleasure,
His latter days in gath'ring treasure;

From superstition liv'd quite free.
And practiced strict morality;
To holy cheats was never willing
To give one solitary shilling:
He can foresee, and for foreseeing
He equals most of men in being,
That Church and State will join their pow'r
And Mis'ry on the country show'r;
And Methodists with their camp bawling,
Will be the cause of this down falling;
An era not destined to see,
It waits for poor posterity.
First fruits and tithes are odious things,
And so are Bishops, Priests, and Kings.

The expertise in the art of composition available to early settlers throughout America is also quite evident in headstone motifs. Often, a cemetery historian may run across simple "folk art" immediately adjacent to elaborate stone carvings of greater detail and elegance. Sometimes, headstones can tell us that local artists influenced other sculptors in outlying regions, as specific designs spread across the landscape and were adopted by apprentice craftsmen. Even in the carving of headstones, therefore, teachers passed their intricate knowledge on to their students.

Much can be learned about a particular stone carver by studying different headstone styles. While continuing research on my own family heritage, I discovered an early American headstone marking the grave of William Sinclair, on which the surname was spelled as "Sinclear." Found standing in a rural churchyard in Spencer, Massachusetts, it clearly exhibits greater expertise than all other stones that surround it. Crafted from a smooth variety of deep blue slate, while those in the immediate vicinity were fashioned from more common schist, it remains in near-mint condition. While the schist stones have split and flaked from aging, making them literally impossible to decipher, the Sinclair marker's incisions still cast keen shadows under bright sunlight.

That portion of the headstone that most captured my attention was the tympanum-topped center section. It displayed an unmistakable skeletal figure in a reclining position, with a soft pillow nestled delicately beneath its head. Who could have carved such an intricate design, and where did this particularly durable slate come from? The answers would not be easy to find, though I was determined to give it my best effort.

After weeks of research in the Central Michigan University library, located just a few miles from where I live, I discovered the

8

stone-carving artistry of one William Codner, who was born on July 24, 1709, in Boston. During his illustrious career, from 1731 until 1764, Codner developed a liking for the human anatomy - more specifically, the skeleton. On numerous occasions, this Massachusetts artist etched deathly skeletons posing in an almost comfortable fashion. Their wide, staring eyes, as well as bone structure, joints, and teeth, were clearly carved.

William Codner's care for detail remains quite evident on the vast majority of his carvings. This was due in large part to his careful choice of materials. In the case of the Sinclair stone, he selected blue slate from nearby Wrentham, Massachusetts, which was then shipped by horse-drawn wagon to Spencer, some thirty miles to the northwest. Thus, I learned a good deal about the death of William Sinclair by studying his gravestone.

In this way, those who spend time wandering about in graveyards are merely visiting this country's outdoor historical museums. After all, they house some of the earliest known examples of memorable poetry and artistic stone carvings. Furthermore, by their very nature, burial spots offer free access to everyone who may be interested in reading American history, viewing American art, or sharing a piece of American heritage. They are a priceless means to educate future generations, as well as to celebrate our culture. Certainly we should not take this available knowledge for granted, for it may be gone tomorrow.

A twelve-foot cross, fashioned from granite, marks the burial site of Wendell L. Wilkie in East Hill Cemetery, Rushville, Indiana. Near the grave is a book-shaped marker which measures more than five feet wide. On its face are fifteen quotes from his campaign speeches, his religious beliefs, and a book entitled *One World.* One small portion explains:

> I believe in America because in it we are free - free to choose our government, to speak our minds, to observe our different religions.
> Because we are generous with our freedom, we share our rights with those who disagree with us.
> Because we hate no people and covet no people's lands.
> Because we are blessed with a natural and varied
> abundance.
> Because we have great dreams and because we have the opportunity to make those dreams come true.

As the graves of our forefathers have begun to show more and more signs of aging, and their inscriptions have become less and less legible, interest in saving them has increased throughout

America. Words of wisdom, such as those inscribed above, deserve that consideration. So let us take a closer look at the origin and progress of America's grave markers. After all, once they have been washed away by time, they will be lost forever.

Chapter 2

American Grave Markers

In Memory of Capt. Hezekiah
Stone, Who Departed this Life
July ye 18th, 1771, in the
61st year of his Age
Beneath this Stone Death's Prisoner lies
the Stone Shall move, the Prisoner Rise.

The typical stone grave marker of today, as the term implies, probably evolved as a means of marking the specific spot where someone had been buried. They were not always used as such, however. Originally, before the entrapping dirt was shoveled in over a coffined corpse, a large, heavy boulder would customarily be placed over its wooden lid. In this way, a stone possessed the dual purpose of protecting the corpse from grave robbers and ensuring that the mortal body would remain peacefully under ground, away from the control of evil spirits. Hence, it seems to have been a simple transition from below-ground to above-ground gravestones.

At times, erection of these more modern surface markers was somewhat haphazard, and could be found in the most unlikely spots. Furthermore, they were not always easily identified as grave markers. The Indian tribes of Nootka Sound, for example, placed a tumulus over their dead, who were normally buried at the crest of a hill. Thereafter, the custom was for a passerby to help construct a monument by simply tossing a stone on the pile. However, as this particular tribe disbanded and died off over generations, their unique burial sites were lost.

As common burial grounds became prevalent in most societies throughout the world, over-crowding soon became a widespread problem. Confusion as to who was buried where began to emerge. Thus, names and dates were inscribed on gravestones for identification purposes. The wealthy, who could afford more lavish

11

funerals, soon became accustomed to erecting extravagant markers to honor their dead. Evidence of this can still be seen in the surviving monuments of the Middle Ages and the ornate tombs of the Renaissance period.

For the peasantry, however, expensive stone markers were simply out of the question. Instead, during the early 17th century, when the first religious refugees fled Europe and came to America, they brought with them the custom of using wood as a suitable substitute. The immigration of several thousand people into the Massachusetts Bay Colony seems to prove this by the shortage of surviving markers predating the 1660's.

The oldest American grave markers lack any type of sculptured or carved designs, and possess only one or two inscibed lines - usually the person's initials, age, and the year that he died. Even this minimal amount of information, however, can sometimes be misleading to people who study early day stones. This is due in large part to the dates: prior to the adoption of the Gregorian calendar in 1752, a great many colonial tombstone makers continued to use the old-styled Julian calendar, while others incorporated the more modern version. Therefore, the inevitable result was much confusion for present-day historians.

During the next several decades, the evolution of grave markers was, for the most part, insignificant. On rare occasions, the day and month were added as a way of pinpointing the time of death. Other than a small amount of insignificant ornamentation along the outside edges of the stone, however, not much else of the accepted design was altered. Hence, these typically crude, thin, square-cornered grave stones remained quite common in early American settlements for several decades.

Eventually, however, from the mid-17th century well into the 18th century, religious beliefs began to dictate a distinct transition in the inherent shape of grave markers. Flat, unadorned slabs were slowly being replaced by carved, vertical memorials, which became known as headstones. Symmetrical in shape, they exhibited curved top center sections which were symbolic of the spiritual transition to eternal life in heaven. Inscriptions were now generally positioned at the center of the stone's face, and a much smaller "footstone" was anchored parallel to the headstone about six feet away. Generally, footstones were much smaller than headstone and, therefore, possessed much less room for inscriptions. As such, if they bore any carving at all it was normally limited to the name or initials of the deceased, perhaps encircled by a simple decorative design. In this way, a particular grave site would be carefully marked and would therefore remain undisturbed by future generations of burials.

12

Other, less common, grave markers were also being used by 17th- and 18th-century Americans. Slabstones, as they were known, were horizontal monuments consisting of a single piece of stone not more than three inches thick and positioned flush with the surface of the surrounding landscape. Inscriptions and border designs were often carved into their flat surface.

Tablestones, or "table tombs," on the other hand, were simply slabstones up to two inches thick that had been elevated to a height of two to three feet by corner leg-supports. These supports, or columns, stood erect on top of a second slabstone set at ground level. Thus, the end result was a gravestone that offered the appearance of a table. In most examples, epitaphs and carvings appeared on the flat surface of the top, and the supporting columns were ornately carved.

Still higher was the tomb, or "boxtomb," which was set off the ground by faced, solid sides. Usually measuring three feet wide, by six feet long, by two to three feet in height, it resembled a simple stone coffin. Most often it marked the grave of an individual; at times, however, it would indicate where an entire family had been buried. A boxtomb should not be confused with the more modern crypt, for interment was below, not above, the ground.

Slabstones, tablestones, and boxtombs remained quite rare, indeed, for none managed to gain the widespread acceptance enjoyed by the more prevalent headstone.

The oldest legibly dated American headstone still standing today can be found in the Palisado Cemetery, located in Windsor, Connecticut, marking the grave of the Reverend Ephraim Huit. A fitting memorial accompanies his name and the inscribed date of 1644:

> sometimes teacher to the church of Windsor:
> who when hee lived, we drew our vitall breath,
> who when hee dyed, his dying was our death.

Further to the northeast, standing in the Old Burying Ground in the seacoast town of Ipswich, Massachusetts, is another stone just three years younger. Though the cemetery was, according to township records, established in 1634, this early marker indicates a fragmented "1647" etched into its face. Finally, in Old Weathersfield, Connecticut, there is a crude dragon carved into the tombstone of Richard Chester, who was buried in 1648. The inscription explains that Chester was an armor bearer, "late of the Town of Blaby and Several other Lordships in Leistersheire."

The historical theory that the stone used to fashion American grave markers such as these was, by and large, imported from

England is most likely untrue. Though this belief persists in a great many written testimonials, it originated and was spread throughout the region by word of mouth. In her book, entitled *Gravestones of Early New England and The Men Who Made Them, 1653-1800*, first published in 1927, Harriette Merrifield Forbes states that, although she "examined hundreds of (ship's) bills," she discovered "no mention of gravestones." She goes on to say that she thoroughly investigated both order-letters addressed to English destinations, as well as local merchant sales records, and could find no evidence of large imports of raw stone or pre-carved gravestones.

More than likely, any shipment of stone slabs imported from Europe was used as ballast, and was later converted into grindstones, building materials, and, occasionally, headstones. It was even more rare, however, for an American buyer to specifically order a custom-made grave marker from England, although specific instances have occurred. A stone marking the grave of Richard Churcher, for example, still stands in the Trinity Churchyard of New York City. The intricately carved monument, dated 1681, was fashioned from stone not native to North America, so it is clear that it originated elsewhere. However, solely from this and other isolated incidents, we cannot in all honesty surmise that the importation of stone was a often-practiced trend.

We can safely say, therefore, that the vast majority of stone materials used for grave markers were found and prepared domestically. In fact, the Reverend Cotton Mather made reference to this fact in 1693 when he said about the epitaph dedicated to Urian Oakes:

> And know, reader, that though the stones in this wilderness are already grown so witty as to speak, they never yet that I could hear of, grew so wicked as to lye.

"The stones in this wilderness" refers to the fact that gravestones came directly from the New England region. And, to further reinforce Mather's statement, geological investigation has proven that the vast majority of early American tombstones came from domestic quarries.

As a collector of tombstone art, it is important to know the various ways in which materials used for gravestones are formed. In general, rocks fall into three genetic classes: igneous, sedimentary, and metamorphic. By understanding their formation, you will better understand step-by-step cleaning and preparatory procedures to use with each type.

Igneous rock is formed when molten material, or "magma," cools and is changed to a hardened, solid state. One example of this would be granite, a name given to a number of different coarse-grained igneous rocks.

Sedimentary rock originates from materials that are gradually deposited at the bottom of the sea, in fresh water lakes, or on land. These materials are normally carried to the area by moving water, heavy winds, or melting ice floes. Furthermore, they may be deposited as either large fragments or as a residue from a liquid solution that has dried or evaporated. Both limestone and sandstone are examples of this type of formation.

Metamorphic rock is classified by the fact that it has undergone some type of change in appearance, density, structure, and in some cases, mineral content. This change takes several thousand years to occur, and is caused by high temperature, intense pressure, or both. The results are quite dramatic, with the rock becoming extremely hard and durable. Examples of this metamorphosis include shale changing into slate, quartz sandstone into quartzite, and limestone into marble.

As has already been stated, when colonists first arrived in America, quarrying rock was not high on their agenda of activities. Hence, they were inclined to use the only material that was readily available for making grave markers: wood. Within a few short years, however, the harsh New England elements caused such markers to weather, fade, and inevitably disintegrate. Hence, within a few decades, settlers were forced to search for a more stable commodity to mark the burial sites of their deceased.

As a solution, townspeople began searching for over-sized common-surface field stones, sometimes referred to as "greenstones," to use as both headstones and footstones. However, these, too, were destined to disappear with the passage of time. Historians believe that as prominent members of the community died and were forgotten, and old families migrated, field stones went unrecognized as grave site monuments and were removed to be used in the foundation construction of homes, barns, court houses, merchant shops, and other buildings.

Eventually, in about 1640, large deposits of sandstone, or siltstone, were discovered and mined, much of which was used for gravestones. Possessing sand-sized granules cemented together naturally by mineral deposits, its sparkling appearance made it appealing to many interested in memorializing deceased relatives. Furthermore, its soft qualities made it quite easy for stone makers to cut and carve.

Eventually, sandstone quarries began to appear in a scattering of regions throughout northeastern America. Along the banks of the Connecticut River, near Windsor, the Hayden Stone Pit was opened for business in the mid-1600's by William Hayden, making it the first of its kind. Hayden "brownstone" was dark brown or reddish brown in color, and was widely used in gravestone bases. In a few areas, it was also fashioned into tablestones and headstones. In fact, this reddish brown variety was used in the aforementioned gravestone of Ephraim Huit.

Later, other large deposits were discovered near towns such as Portland and Chatham, which offered deep red, light tan, and even rich chocolate varieties of sandstone. Soon thereafter, advertisements for sandstone monuments began to appear throughout the region. Shaler and Hall promised to "deliver them at any Port in North America." Being highly abundant for decades to come made this type of stone, without a doubt, the most widely used substance for memorials to the dead.

Today, epitaph historians, genealogists, and collectors will have an extremely difficult time deciphering inscriptions on the majority of sandstone grave markers. One type, known commonly as bluestone because of its fine-grained dark green or bluish gray color, was particularly vulnerable to erosion. Not only did these soft bluestone markers wear easily, but they tended to split apart and chip as the rain, snow, and ice worked its way deep within its crevices. In essence, many sandstone markers, left miserably unprotected from the elements, were destined to literally rot from the inside out.

On the other hand, some quarry sites--such as one located in Longmeadow, Massachusetts, as well as others throughout the Connecticut Valley--provided a high grade of sandstone that has endured quite well over the years. The headstone of William Wells, who was buried in 1696 in Southold, Long Island, is just such an example, for the afternoon sun still casts deep shadows within its incisions. If you do happen to encounter others like this, which are still fairly legible, do not hesitate to record them in some way; most likely, they will not last forever.

In searching for your buried relatives, you may on occasion discover headstones fashioned from a soft rock known as soapstone. Not to be confused with sandstone, it contains a high concentration of talc. While examining stones cut from this material, do not be surprised if the entire inscription, as well as the original shape of the marker, has been drastically altered.

During the late 18th- and early 19th-centuries, the most commonly used stone for grave markers was a soft, dark slate that was unearthed from quarry sites situated throughout the northeastern portions of America. Later, from Cambridge and Slate Island, Massachusetts, came a more durable, light-colored variety that was crossed by white bands; from the Narragansett Basin, sandwiched between Massachusetts and Providence, Rhode Island, came a cameo of hard, rosy-green slate; and in the Wrentham, Massachusetts region originated a wide array of highly-polished color combinations, including yellow, orange, green, rose, blue, gray, and black.

Ordinarily, slate headstones withstood the test of time, due to their inherent formative qualities. Made up in large part of clay minerals, it was toughened and hardened over centuries. Eventually it dried, changing from its original clay into an extremely stable natural stone. On occasion, however, if it was mined before its time, the result would be a headstone fashioned from more vulnerable, brittle shale, which would readily split away in complete layers.

For the epitaph collector, multi-colored slate headstones will provide spectacular photographs. Their years of exposure to the sun, wind, and rain have not seemed to cause a fading effect, for they continue to retain their brilliant hues. However, during this period the stonemakers incorporated an Italic-type script for their headstone lettering. Such engraving, due to its unfamiliar style and shallow incisions, is extremely difficult to see and read.

During this same period of time, a few stone-makers preferred to reach toward this "cameo" effect through the use of a variety of quartzite intermingled with layers of black hornblende. Found primarily in the area around Belchertown, Massachusetts, just a dozen miles or so northeast of Springfield, the result was a swirled mixture of gray, black, and white. On occasion, however, brighter combinations of yellow, red, and purple were discovered, making for a unique blend of coloration.

As described before, quartzite is an altered type of quartz sandstone. During its formation, high temperature and high pressure cause a second layer of quartz crystals to form around the small, sandy grains. Though it looks somewhat similar to its cousin, in reality quartzite is much denser and harder than ordinary sandstone. Therefore in most cases, the accidental end result of using the colorful quartzite to fashion markers was that they were able to stand up better to the harsh New England weather. Many centuries-old headstones fashioned from quartzite look as if they were carved within the past few years.

Still, when used in damp climates, a great number of cracks will prevail on quartzite grave markers. As a result, similar cracks will be prevalent on a finished rubbing as well, making it quite difficult to distinguish between intended incisions and those that have resulted haphazardly with the passage of time. Perhaps, if you wish to preserve these epitaphs and artwork, careful gravestone tracing, as described in Chapter 8, will offer the best results.

In the northern Massachusetts county of Essex, near the Merrimack River basin, stone cutters began to use a type of schist for local headstones during the late 1700's. Once again, legibility is a problem, for the lettering on such stones is quite difficult to discern. Further to the east, in the seacoast county of Plymouth, epitaph researchers will encounter other difficulties with schist. There, a green-colored variety was used to cut hundreds of headstones, which have since cracked and decayed beyond recognition. If, in the course of your genealogical search, you find direct descendants that lived in this region, you may be discouraged by the splintered headstone remnants that you encounter.

Near Bolton, Connecticut, a variety of mica schist, known as Bolton Stone, became popular in the production of headstones. This, too, is quite difficult to read, although a number of these seem to have survived the inland ravages of snow and ice. Possessing a uniqueness all its own, Bolton Stone emits a sparkling image, offering the illusion of a vast array of gold and fine cut gems inset amid clear crystal when bathed in bright sunlight.

Another common material used in the manufacture of headstones during the colonial period was limestone, a sedimentary variety of rock composed mainly of calcite, dolimite, or both. Although not as hard, it is often mistaken for marble, and withstands a good deal of invasion from the elements. Photographers will, undoubtedly, be happy with the results of their artwork while taking shots of its deep, shadowy incisions.

Marble gravestones remained unheard of until the end of the 17th century, when it was first discovered by Colonel James Noyes in Newbury, Massachusetts. Still, prior to intensive mining efforts throughout the region, anyone desiring a marble monument was forced to order it from England. Such was the case with William Pepperell, who purchased a headstone for his father in 1737. Specifically, he wanted "a handsome marble tomb-stone with proper marble pillars or supporters to set it on."

Exploitation of marble remained, for the most part, inactive until the late 18th century. In areas such as southwestern Vermont, near Proctor, for example, the world's deepest marble quarries were discovered. Primarily white and gray in color, it was extremely durable and relatively easy to inscribe. With it came the return of Roman lettering, and epitaph readers of today can see fine samples of it, dating from 1760, still standing in the Old Burying Ground of Bennington, Vermont.

During the second half of the 19th century, granite was being quarried in southern Connecticut--primarily from the community of Norwich--and this was also used in shaping head-stones. Other regions throughout eastern America soon followed, and freshly carved granite became the preferred choice.

However, for the epitaph collector, this new type of stone was accompanied by a new epitaph and sculpturing fashion: instead of incised carvings, raised lettering and designs became popular. Unfortunately, this is often as troublesome to read and decipher as engraving, particularly if the light is not ample or lichens have grown over the stone. If you, as a genealogical researcher, hope to get a clear photograph (rubbing and tracing are definitely out) of this variety, a sound cleaning is advised. Making a foiling (see Chapter 11), on the other hand, may be your wisest choice.

More recently, during the onset of the 20th century, monument makers started incorporating a substance known as artificial stone for their artwork. It includes such varieties as art marble, artificial marble, cast stone, and composite stone, each of which is man-made by mixing stone chips or fragments with cement or plaster. With brilliant fragments embedded in the compound, the hardened stone is then ground down, polished, and etched.

Those who browse through graveyards and cemeteries throughout the United States may find samples of headstones fashioned from field boulders, soapstone, sandstone, schist, quartzite, granite, shale, slate, marble, or artificial stone. Keep in mind, however, that unique epitaphs and carvings have more to do with the time period than with the location. If, for example, your genealogical records indicate that your ancestor died before 1850, you very well may find a hand-carved, locally composed epitaph upon his or her headstone. However, if your relative was buried during the latter half of the 19th century, it is more likely that you'll discover one with no epitaph, and very little creatively carved originality.

It was during this era that the Industrial Revolution took a firm hold on American lifestyle. White marble memorials, emblazoned with typical urns and willows, became widespread. Hand incisions were also destined to become a thing of the past, being replaced by more innovative sandblasting procedures. The results were devastating to art lovers: uniform, repeated symbols of urns and willows created a monotonous type of cemetery. And, as monument manufacturing companies were established all across the country, even gravestone artwork of this manufactured sort would not last long.

Still, despite the invasion of technology, a few artists did indeed persist. As far west as the Ohio-Indiana state line, for example, a wide array of valuable epitaphs and gravestone carvings can be found in pockets settled by Eastern colonists. Furthermore, during the 20th century, hand-carved inscriptions and sculpturing techniques seem to be making a welcome comeback. It just goes to prove that tradition survives as long as the modern culture invites it to do so.

In more recent times, during the 20th century, cement grave markers have replaced artistic monuments of the past. Hubert Eaton, who in 1917 became the manager of the Forest Lawn Memorial-Park Cemetery, located in Los Angeles, California, had visions of refurbishing the run-down, weed-infested burial ground. He held a serene picture in his mind of a cemetery "filled with towering trees, sweeping lawns, splashing fountains, singing birds, beautiful statues, cheerful flowers, noble memorial archetecture...where memorialization of loved ones in sculptured marble and pictorial glass shall be encouraged..."

Eventually Eaton, like many of his contemporaries, was forced to admit that the elimination of tombstones would be a wise gesture for the sake of space. In time, Forest Lawn began to replace them with small, insignificant bronze markers. However, Eaton later agreed that the old-styled headstone was a "great assist" to one aspect of the more conventional cemeteries of the past. The "great assist," as he put it, that was discarded was the time-honored epitaph. There just wasn't enough room for such poetic inscriptions on Forest Lawn's 12-by-24-inch bronze markers.

Progress, though it has altered the likelihood of quaint and curious epitaphs for future generations, can still be redirected. In fact, Eaton himself once claimed that the epitaph was on the verge of making a dramatic comeback. He suggested the creation of "ever-larger" bronze tablets all across America, "big enough to contain complete epitaphs and historical data - big enough to cover the entire grave!" Yet, to fully understand epitaphs of the future, we must first begin by understanding epitaphs of the past.

Chapter 3

The History of Epitaphs

This modest stone, what few vain marbles can,
May truly say, Here lies an honest man:
Calmly he looked on either life and here
Saw nothing to regret or there to fear.

An epitaph is defined as "an inscription on a tomb, written in prose or verse, in commemoration of one who is buried." The term comes to us from two Greek words: "epi," meaning "upon," and "taphos," meaning "tomb." Originally, these gravestone inscriptions were designed as a simple historical means of perpetuating a person's name, birthday, and death date. Yet, as time went by, a great deal of additional information was also included. Pious thoughts, which reflected a person's life, were etched into stones; words of wisdom and warning were written for the reading pleasure of the living; and a line or two concerning personal characteristics often were added for the sake of heritage. Hence, tombstone inscriptions began to evolve and change because of a desire for man to move toward nonconformity, and each individual gravestone became somewhat different from the next.

The origin of epitaph commemoration is difficult to pinpoint. William Camden (1551-1623), famed English antiquarian who founded the Camden professorship of history at Oxford, attempted to trace the history of tombstone inscriptions. After years of research, he concluded that the ancient scholars of Theban mythology, while mourning the death of the musician/poet Linus, "fyrst bewayled theyre master, when he was slayne, in doleful verse." Such verses were referred to as "epitaphia," which were initially sung by mourners at the time of the burial.

The Bible, on the other hand, would have us believe that headstone inscriptions have been around since the very beginning of human existence. One passage tells us of the "great stone of

21

Abel," a monument placed over the tomb by Adam, his father. The epitaph read: "Here was shed the blood of the righteous Abel."

Whatever the origin of the epitaph might be, tombstone inscriptions came about as a means of preserving the memory of the deceased. The earliest known epitaphs were written by ancient Egyptian scholars long before the birth of Christ. There, names, royal blood lines, and titles of nobility belonging to the dead were inscribed upon individual sarcophagi and stone coffins.

The Greeks, who were responsible for the birth of epitaphs in verse, wrote simple, dignified memorial passages to the dead. One example can be found on a monument dedicated to the Spartans who forfeited their lives in the defense of their country. Translated into English it reads:

> Go tell the Spartans, thou that passest by,
> That here obedient to their laws we lie.

Later, during imperial times in the Roman empire, simple expressions of praise were written on the tombs of the dead, along with the name, station in life, and age at the time of death. Most often, instead of a more personal memory, a brief description of acts of public service was offered: the construction of cities, important battle victories, and other types of community involvement. Dr. Samuel Johnson (1709-1784), famed British writer, lexicographer, and author of the *Dictionary of the English Language*, had this to say on the subject of ancient epitaph writing:

> Nature and reason have dictated to every nation
> that to preserve good actions from oblivion is both the
> interest and duty of mankind. No people acquainted with
> the use of letters [have failed] to grace the tombs of their
> heroes and wise men with panegyrical inscriptions.

Ancient Rome was responsible for the origin of tombstone inscriptions in the form of a curse, used to warn grave robbers against violation of the deceased's remains. Other cultures soon followed suit. In fact, those who visit the grave of William Shakespeare at the Holy Trinity Church in Stratford-on-Avon are often surprised to see the following words:

> Good frend for Iesvs sake forbeare,
> To dig the dvst encloased heare!
> Bleste be ye man yt spares thes stones,
> And curst be he yt moves my bones.

Indeed, however, the inscription was placed there during an era when grave robbery was almost inevitable. Furthermore, the curse must have done its job: although a number of nearby graves were violated, Shakespeare's went untouched.

As time went by, a man or woman's occupation was added to the inscription: a Roman who sold pigs for a living was not ashamed to tell the world of his trade; a clown of the city company of mountebanks was remembered for his playful antics; and a baker's final resting place was constructed in the form of an oven, including his loaves, kneading trough, and mill. We find the following over the remains of a man who was given the shameful distinction of being the one responsible for inventing spectacles:

> Here lies Sagvino Armalo D'Armati,
> of Florence,
> the inventor of spectacles.
> May God pardon his sins!
> The year 1318.

From the first to the sixth century A.D., a variety of poetic Christian inscriptions evolved. It should not be surprising, therefore, that references to the Bible and books of devotional verse were often used to memorialize the deceased:

> If heaven be pleased when sinners cease to sin,
> If hell be pleased when sinners enter in,
> If earth be pleased when ridded of a knave,
> Then all are pleased, for Coleman's in his grave.

The tradition of composing epitaphs soon caught on in western portions of Europe, particularly England. A great many of these inscriptions, however, were not rooted in Christian beliefs. Instead, they tended to commemorate a person's station in life or occupation. For example, a large church congregation remembered its organ player in Bluntsham, 1621 with the following:

> Under this stone lies Meredith Morgan
> Who blew the bellows of our Church Organ:
> Tobacco he hated, to smoke most unwilling,
> Yet never so pleased as when pipes he was filling;
> No reflection on him for rude speech could be cast,
> Tho' he gave our old organ many a blast.

The following epitaph can still be seen in Gateshead, Durham, over the remains of an architect:

Here lies Robert Trollope,
Who made yon stones roll up;
When death took his soul up,
His body filled this hole up.

And, we find a punning inscription over the grave of an Irish grocer:

Here lie the remains of John Hall, grocer,
The world is not worth a fig, and I have
good raisins for saying so.

During the early 1600's, stinging criticism of the dead became prevalent thoughout Europe. An exmple of this satirical type of expression can be found over the remains of Alexander Pope, famous English poet:

Here lies Lord Corningsby - be civil.
The rest God knows; so does the devil.

In America, tombstone inscriptions originated during the mid-17th century. At that time, extensive epitaph writing was not yet being carried out, as is proven by the numerous gravestones that simply had the intitials of the deceased along with the year of his or her death. This was destined to change, however, within a few short decades.

It was during the mid-1670's that Latin phrases became prevalent on American monuments, for they began to appear in the Massachusetts Bay Colony. They included such well-known words as *Memento mori* ("Remember that you must die"), *Memento te esse mortalem* ("Remember that you are mortal"), and *Fugit hora* ("The hour is fleeting"). Such epitaphs were inscribed, for the most part, only within the immediate New England region until the first decade of the 18th century. Then, gradually they began to spill over into other distant colonies and settlements, as far west as the Ohio Valley and as far south as Georgia.

It is important to understand why such descriptive verses became popular in early New England society. During the 17th and 18th centuries, the Puritan way of life was, by law, simple and unadorned. Homes, tableware, furniture, and clothing were plain, yet useful; originality, creativity and decoration were forbidden. This carried over, in fact, to paintings and other wall decorations of the times. Simply put, their strict religious concept did not allow conscious expression or individuality in life.

Puritan meetinghouses and churches, therefore, because of their forbidding beliefs, were sacred sanctuaries and free of all imagery. Holidays were not celebrated, church decoration was not allowed, and songs were not sung. In essence, as one writer put it, "the secular life was not allowed to intrude on the sanctity of these buildings."

Despite the rigid regulations governing decorative pomp in day-to-day living and religious ceremony, the Puritan burial grounds were a different matter. Since they were situated outside of Puritan jurisdiction, it was conceded that they were under the control of the general population. Therefore, freedom of expression in the form of tombstone inscription and art was allowed. Despite this small liberty, however, epitaphs were not aimed at memorializing the dead; they were intended to be an educational experience for the living.

Burial grounds, therefore, became a solemn place for one to peacefully sit, read, and contemplate what he or she could learn from headstone inscriptions. Entire families, including young children, were encouraged to partake in these important lessons. Furthermore, such inscriptions undoubtedly offered the largely illiterate congregations an opportunity to practice the art of reading. And, in the process, they often came away with a more formidable understanding of Puritan morals than they were able to secure from the intensely symbolic religious sermons of the day.

Although the practice of epitaph writing is no longer being extensively carried out, except in rare cases upon the monuments of famous people, there once was a time in America when it was an extremely popular custom. Quotes were borrowed from the Bible and collections of devotional verse; professional epitaph writers composed them for hire; amateur poets wrote them for friends and relatives; and village clergymen, schoolmasters, or tombstone makers supplied them when no other source was readily available.

Often, ingenuity was far more important than excellence in skill when it came to writing a person's epitaph. Therefore in a number of cases, the resulting inscription comes across as being either ludicrous, unbecoming, inept, or sometimes even humorous:

To the Memory of
Abraham Beaulieu
Born 15 September 1822
Accidentally shot
4th April 1844
As a mark of affection
from his brother.

Despite this obviously accidental play on words, which has transformed a serious memorial into one of humor, we have still managed to learn something of Abraham Beaulieu: his age, birthday, death day, cause of death, and who was responsible for dedicating the headstone. Hence every bit and piece of knowledge left behind, whether accurate or misleading, seems to contribute to the total picture of a person's livelihood. Therefore, anyone aspiring to collect epitaphs--whether for a personal genealogical record or knowledge of general American heritage--must regard it as an important and worthwhile pursuit.

Though such is not the case with the above epitaph, most tombstone inscriptions are, because of their historical nature, of an obscure origin with no known author, and may cover a wide variety of topics. A special memory might include a specific conversation or a repulsive bad habit; it may be an act of heroism or foolishness; or it may be nothing more than a singular memory retained by family, friends, or neighbors.

While studying the tombstones which have survived the test of time, you might notice that many are quite similar. In fact, they may even be exactly alike, including poor grammar and spelling errors. From this, you might reach the logical conclusion that in centuries past originality of composition was seldom thought to be important. The copying of epitaphs within a single cemetery suggests that petty plagiarism was widespread during past generations. A typical verse, paraphrased extensively in a number of early New England graveyards, reads:

> What I was once some may relate,
> What I am now is each one's fate;
> What I shall be none can explain,
> Till he that called, call again.

Perhaps the theft of another person's epitaph was not the case after all, for few people today realize that tombstone inscriptions were at one time published in a wide variety of books. One such text, printed in England, was entitled: *The Epitaph-Writer: Consisting of Upwards of Six Hundred Original Epitaphs, Moral, Admonitory, Humorous, and Satirical: Numbered, Classed, and Arranged, on a New Plan: Chiefly Designed for Those Who Write or Engrave Inscriptions on Tombstones* (Chester, 1791). The author, John Bowden, offered four steadfast rules for the composition of tombstone poetry: (1) "It is highly necessary that the Praise bestowed on the Dead should be restrained within the Bounds of Truth," (2) the inscription should be of interest to the reader, for "without this an Epitaph can be little more than a Piece of unpardonable Vanity; at best it can be but a dead, uninteresting narrative, if not a mere Landmark," (3) "The serious reflections should be written in as lively and striking a manner as possible....so as to awaken and engage the Attention of the Thoughtless, and alarm the Fears of the Vicious and Guilty," and (4) be brief and to the point in order to reflect "the Design of the Writer and the necessary Information and Good of the Reader."

Another book, entitled *The Silver Stole, being a collection of One Hundred Texts of Scripture: and One Hundred Original Epitaphs, suitable for The Grave of a Child,* was written by J. W. Cummings in 1859. Today, a great number of these epitaphs can still be found on tombstones throughout the country, including:

> 'Tis but the casket that lies here,
> The gem that filled it sparkles yet.

An in-depth study of the many epitaphs that survive throughout America today provides us with touches of local and national histories, personal biographies, religious beliefs, human behavior, and poetic literature. Upon these remaining weathered stone monuments we see commentaries on lost love, bittersweet marriage, Heavenly paradise, enduring friendship, Hell's damnation, the evils of money, and occupational hazards. Types of expression include the serene, the devout, the ridiculous, the pompous, and the quaint:

> I will awake, O Christ, when thou callest me, but
> let me sleep awhile - for I am very weary....

We have no way of determining precisely when graveyard humor first became an accepted way of commemorating the dead. *The Greek Anthology* offers a wide variety of examples that date back to classical times, which exhibit very little in the way of solemn thought. Yet, since religion has long played a part in burial ceremonies, we might assume that such beliefs were the basis of our earliest tombstone wit. And, ever since, we have been "blessed" with a long list of unforgettable epitaphs. On the subject of Hell, for example, we find the following epitaph, which possesses a distinctly humorous flavor:

> Beneath this plain pine board is lying
> The body of Joshua Hight,
> "Cheer up," the parson told him, dying;
> "Your future's very bright."
> Slowly the sick man raised his head,

27

His weeping friends amazing.
"Parson, it's most too bright," he said,
"For I can see it blazing!"

Next, we have a "monstrous" gentleman attempting to enter Heaven's gate. Though the inscription fails to record the cause of his death, it dwells on an unusual physical feature:

Here lies a man of good repute
Who wore a No. 16 boot
'Tis not recorded how he died,
But sure it is that open wide
The gates of heaven must have been
To let such monstrous feet within.

Finally, it seems rather obvious where this man's friends and relatives believed he ended up:

John burns.

In the tiny hamlet of Pembroke, Massachusetts, nestled eight miles inland from the north shore of Plymouth Bay, a grave marker sums up the life of a housewife and mother. Life for her was quite obviously a tremendous struggle; and, even more clear was the fact that she looked forward to a better existence in the next world:

Here lies a poor woman who always was tired,
She lived in a house where help wasn't hired.
The last words she said were "Dear friends, I am going,
Where washing ain't wanted, nor mending, nor sewing.
There all things is done exact to my wishes,
For where folks don't eat there's no washing of dishes.
In heaven loud anthems forever are ringing,
But having no voice, I'll keep clear of the singing.
Don't mourn for me now, don't mourn for me never;
I'm going to do nothing, forever and ever."

Whatever portrait we may hold dearly in our minds, we should remember that commemorative memories of the dead are, indeed, the by-product of a very real relationship. One wonders what future archeologists and epitaph historians will think of our world today. Though one of the more interesting aspects of current research is that headstone inscriptions provide a number of clues to the customs and peculiarities of the past, we cannot help but be concerned as to what clues our headstones will offer later generations. For a better understanding of our present-day concept of death and the afterlife, perhaps twenty-fourth century antiquarians should recall the words of Andrew Marvell, a poet who had much to say about modern attitudes:

> The grave's a fine and private place,
> But none, I think, do there embrace.

Keeping this is mind, let us "embrace" a brief collection of humorous, quaint, and curious epitaphs from America's past, for if we allow 16th-, 17th-, and 18th-century burial grounds to remain a "private place," we will lose an important piece of history forever.

Chapter 4

Quaint, Curious, & Educational

American Epitaphs

In memory of
Capt. Thomas Stetson
Who was killed by the fall of
a tree Nov. 28 1820 AE. 68
Nearly 30 years he was master
of a vessel and left that
employment at the age of
48 for the less hazardous
one of cultivating his farm.
Man is never secure from
the arrest of death.

While snooping through aging American cemeteries in search of long-lost relatives or worthwhile inscriptions for your collection, you will undoubtedly discover a variety of quaint, curious, and educational tombstone memories. As I have already stated, there are a number of people throughout the country today who feel that it shows disrespect for the dead to find anything enjoyable within a graveyard. Still, I believe that this somewhat outdated attitude is changing. After all, epitaphs are dedicated to thousands of people who enjoyed living, and most likely they would approve of others finding a little enjoyment over their graves.

In perusing tombstone literature, you will find inscriptions that cover a wide range of topics and a wide range of moods. You may, for example, see a small memorial written about the Civil War which is presented in a patriotic fashion. Nearby, on another stone, you might come across a few words dedicated to a person's family, with the words expressing sarcasm. Finally, over an adjacent grave you may read a small slice of wisdom concerning death itself, composed with a bit of mystery and intrigue. Hence, keep one thing in mind as you search through forgotten cemeteries: a tombstone investigator should always expect the unexpected.

Religion, perhaps more than any other facet of human life, played a key role in our ancestor's lives. Our forefathers came here hoping to find religious freedom; the ideal behind their search became part of our First Amendment rights, and hundreds of churches flourished during our nation's first two centuries. With that in mind, we should take a close look at a selection of epitaphs that speak to us of God, the devil, heaven, and hell.

One of the most commonly used verses etched into headstones during colonial times was a variation of the following:

> Such as thou art,
> Sometime was I,
> Such as I am,
> Such shalt thou be.

This familiar phrasing was initially used in England in 1376 on the tomb of Edward, the Black Prince, in Canterbury Cathedral, Canterbury, England. Later, it was rewritten and paraphrased throughout New England and beyond, with a typical version reading:

> Traveler, pause as you pass by,
> As you are now, so once was I;
> As I am now, so you shall be,
> Prepare for Death and follow me.

And still another:

> Death is a debt
> By nature due:
> I've paid my shot,
> And so must you.

Social life in early Puritan New England townships was somewhat restrictive. Enjoyment was limited to eating, sleeping, attending church, and having an occasional conversation with neighbors. Perhaps for that reason, and because conducting a funeral and burial service was such a familiar occurrence, celebrating them through poetic inscriptions was a natural defense against the fear of dying. In 1683, following the deaths of two of his four children, Edward Taylor composed the following inscription:

Christ would in glory have a Flower, Choice, Prime, and
having Choice, chose this my branch forth brought. Lord
take it. I thank thee thou takest ought of mine, it is
my pledge in glory.

In a second verse addressing death, Taylor wrote:

Why camest thou then so slowly? Mend thy pace.
Thy slowness me detains from Christ's bright face.
Although thy terrors rise to the highest degree,
I am still where I was. A fig for thee!

Hence, it seems quite obvious that some form of "life after
death" was thought to be in the future for everyone. Most believed
that they were destined for a "better place," as seen on a headstone
in Ithaca, New York:

While on earth my knee was lame,
I had no nurse and heed it.
But now I've gone to a better place
Where I do not even need it.

In Lewis Cemetery, Bemus Point, New York, is this odd inscription
to Belvera Annis, who was buried in 1841:

Tho' greedy worms devour my skin
And gnaw my wasting flesh
When God shall build my bones again
He'll clothe them all afresh.

And the following quaint words, though barely legible on a cracked
and weathered slate stone, can still be read in Old North Cemetery,
Nantucket, Massachusetts:

Under the sod
Under these trees
Lies the body of Jonathan Pease
He is not here
But only his pod
He has shelled out his peas
And gone to his God.

Yet, on more than one occasion, we discover that the living
were often unsure of the destination of the deceased. Such were

the feelings expressed over the remains of Charles A. Miller, who was buried in Vineland, New Jersey:

> I came I know not wence,
> I go I know not whither.

In Adams Cemetery, Barre Plains, Massachusetts, is another verse dedicated to the vagueness of destination:

> Husband farewell, a long farewell
> And children all adieu
> And when we meet no tongue can tell
> How I shall welcome you.

Another common sentiment was one in which the relatives literally "pointed" out the destination of the deceased by inscribing a finger extending either up toward the heavens or down toward hell. One amusing passage, found etched into a headstone just beneath a finger extending in the downward direction, commented that the deceased had "gone home to be reunited with friends."

A more modern version, which poses an amusing poetic question, was found in the Ohio Valley:

> Which way did he go? Which way did he go?
> Up above, or down below?

In studying tombstone literature, you will likely notice that an abundance of descriptive, personal characteristics have been bestowed upon the dead. They include such qualities as "pure," "loving," "peaceable," "honorable," "amiable," "virtuous," "charitable," and "dutiful." In fact, as you continue to read, you may begin to see that such repetitive, almost ultra-human qualifiers were used far too often. Quite obviously, competition among local townsfolk grew to intense proportions during the 18th and 19th centuries, all in a futile effort to bestow unforgettable and almost unbelievable traits upon the lifestyles of the deceased. In Farmington, Connecticut, for instance, we find an inscription that was quite typical of the times:

> Here Lieth Interr'd the Body of Mr. Noah Andruss:
> Graduated at Yale College, A.D. 1777, & Departed this
> life of ye 29th of May, 1780: a young gentleman of good
> geniuses, an accomplished Scholar, evangelical preachur,
> amiable friend, & exhibited a bright example of ye
> virtues, & graces of ye Christian character.

Such redundant attributes, although touching, are not easily imprinted in our memories, simply because the vast majority seem so repetitive. From time to time, however, you will discover an epitaph that possesses originality, as well as a hint of competitiveness. In a rural New England graveyard, for example, I found the following comparitive inscription over the grave of a middle-aged gentleman:

Here I lie, snug as a bug in a rug.

In an adjacent plot, a rather jealous relative had made an avid attempt at outdoing him by writing:

Here I lie, snugger than that other bugger.

Throughout the annals of history, brave men have lived and died for their country, their family, and their friends. And, from the very beginning, Americans were no different than their forefathers. In King's Chapel Burying Ground, for example, which was established soon after the founding of Boston, Massachusetts, one can find a great many epitaphs commemorating heroism. From the faint words on a stone marking the grave of an early-day soldier, we discover that "he was a hopeful gent and an experienced soldier and buryed with military funeral."

This curious tale is preserved on a tablet in Christ Church, Boston, Massachusetts:

Major John Pitcairn
Fatally wounded
while rallying the Royal Marines
at the Battle of Bunker Hill
was carried from the field to the boats
on the back of his son
who kissed him and returned to duty.

Abner Baker, who was hanged as a spy in 1865, is buried in First Presbyterian Churchyard, Knoxville, Tennessee, with the following epitaph on his gravestone:

A martyr for manliness and personal rights.
His death was an honor to himself but an
everlasting disgrace to his enemies.
Cowards die many times
The brave but once!

Probably the most widely known military tribute is that which appears over the grave of the Unknown Soldier in Arlington, Virginia:

Here Rests in
Honored Glory
An American Soldier
Known But to God.

Similarly, as with soldiers, sailors were often honored for their brave exploits. The epitaph of Captain George Fred Tilton, who died in 1932, is a prime example:

Whaleman
who
in 1897 walked 3380 miles
through Alaskan winter to
save the lives of 200 men
on four whaleships caught
in Arctic ice.

In 1863, Charles H. Petty was commemorated by his shipmates, who recalled that "his death occured in nine hours after being bitten by a shark, while bathing near the ship."

All across America, people have long taken pride in their stations in life, and often speak of occupations on their headstones. For the genealogist, such an inscription can offer a bit of insight into an ancestor's career, as well as his feelings toward life. When Al Shean, a member of the Vaudville duo of Gallagher and Shean, was buried in Mount Pleasant Cemetery, Pleasantville, New York, he was memorialized with the following lines from their act:

I could have lived longer
But now it's too late
Absolutely Mr. Gallagher -
Positively Mr. Shean.

In Newport, Rhode Island, there is a headstone over the remains of Isaac Thurstone that is fashioned in the shape of a log. Attached is an inscription which reads:

He sawed logs for forty years
But he won't saw this one.

36

In New York City, Thial Clark compared his own lifelong occupation to what he hoped for after death:

> In memory of
> Thial Clark, the jeweler, who has
> quit running, but is wound up in
> the hopes of being taken by the
> hand by the Supreme Master machinist
> for repairs and to be adjusted
> and set running for the world to
> come again.

Situated in the Gate of Heaven Cemetery, in Hawthorne, New York, is a monument commemorating George Herman (Babe) Ruth, who died at the age of 53 in 1948. Etched into a side panel is an inscription that reads:

> May the Divine Spirit
> That Animated
> Babe Ruth
> To win the Crucial
> Game of Life
> Inspire the Youth
> Of America.

At times, occupation was not nearly as important as expressing the a single memory of the deceased. Hence, heart-felt opinions often took the place of life-long human endeavors, as people spoke of final justice:

> He found a rope and picked it up,
> And with it walked away.
> It happened that to the other end
> A horse was hitched, they say.
> They took the rope and tied it up
> Unto a hickory limb.
> It happened that the other end
> Was somehow hitched to him.

Apparently, in the mind of Richard C.S. Pond, there were a number of redeeming qualities to living poor on the farm rather than rich in the city. His experience was expressed on a common field boulder, with many plow scratches, just outside of Milford, Connecticut:

Who among you plow boys ever associated the blow of
the plow point on the hidden stone as one of happiness?
Not one of you until you have tasted the dissapointments,
sorrows and rottenness of yonder city.

Uncountable married partners have taken it upon themselves to inscribe a memory over the graves of their dearly departed. Although the vast majority of epitaphs composed by spouses
describe love and loss, others express relief that the marriage had
reached an end. Such was the case of the inscription marking the
joint grave of Obadiah and Ruth Wilkinson, which bluntly states
that "their warfare is accomplished." Another example, commemorating a woman from Burlington, Vermont, spoke of a happier life
ahead:

> She lived with her husband fifty years
> And died in the confident hope
> of a better life.

A great number of spouses outlived their married partners
by many years. In Bradford, Massachusetts, a stone marker was
erected to commemorate Nathanial Thurstone, who finally met his
match in 1811. In a row beside him stand a half-dozen slate
stones, praising six of his seven wives.

Even in death, spouses were quite fearful of telling un-
truths concerning their real feelings. After all, "speaking the Devil's words" would, undoubtedly, lead one straight to the doors of
Hell. Such honesty in death is evidenced by an epitaph from a
vindictive husband:

> Here lies my wife,
> A Slattern and Shrew.
> If I said I missed her,
> I should lie here, too!

A huge monument dedicated to Mathies G. Braden in Old Manden
Cemetery bears the following odd message:

> Stranger call this not a place
> Of Fear and Gloom.
> To me it is a pleasant spot,
> It is my husbands tomb.

Side-by-side markers in an old Pennsylvania church yard repre-
sents a splendid dialogue between husband and wife:

Woman:

"Grieve not for me my husband dear
I am not dead, but sleeping here;
With patience wait, prepare to die
And, in a short time, you'll come to I."

Man:

"I am not grieved, my dearest life
Sleep on, I've found another wife.
Therefore, I cannot come to thee
For I must go and live with she."

Expressing a similar sentiment, a widower placed the following message on his wife's gravestone:

1890 - The Light of my Life has gone out.

A single year later, the following was added:

1891 - I have struck another match.

Despite their great loss, and their anxiety to fill the void in their lives, widows and widowers alike were not always fortunate to find another to take the place of the deceased. Many subsequently lived on, alone, up to forty years or more. Yet, though her efforts went unrewarded, one young woman did not give up trying, and even advertised on her husband's gravestone in Lincoln, Maine:

Sacred to the memory of Mr. Jared
Bates who died Aug. the 6th 1800.
His widow aged 24 who mourns as
one who can be comforted lives at
7 Elm Street, this village, and
possesses every qualification for
a Good Wife.

Then there are those who don't quite make it to the altar. In fact, confirmed bachelors from Plymouth, Massachusetts, may have believed that James Jordan was spared from a fate worse than death when he "Drowned in a Smelt Pot" and was "Buried on the day he was to have been Married." A monument that still stands in a Providence, Rhode Island, graveyard relates a similar tale:

Sidney Snyder, 1823,
age 20
The wedding day decided
The wedding wine provided;

But ere the day did come along
He'd drunk it up and died did.
Ah Sidney! Ah Sidney!

During the mid- and late-1800's, it was common practice for entire families to stroll leisurely among the neat rows of weathered, lichen-covered headstones, deciphering epitaphs, and copying choice inscriptions. Most often, words marking the grave of a prominent citizen, a close relative, or a neighbor were preferred over the unusual, curious, or odd. Periodically, however, a detailed account of one's accidental passing was found; a young man who had "exploded in a powder mill"; a graphic account of a farmer "at a barn raising (who) fell down from the roof"; and one who was overcome by the whims of temptation:

That Cherry Tree of luscious fruit
beguiled him too high. A branch did
break and down he fell and broke his
neck.

In a sarcastic vein, the husband of Ellen Shannon hoped to warn others of an unfortunate accident in Girard, Pennsylvania:

In memory of
Ellen Shannon
Aged 26 gears
Who was fatally burned
March 21st 1870
by the explosion of a lamp
filled with "R. E. Danforth's
Non Explosive
Burning Fluid"

With the beginning of the Industrial Revolution, the workplace was often the site of terrible accidents. An account of one such incident was chiselled into the stone of Solomon Towslee, Jr., who:

....was kill'd in Pownal, Vt., July
15, 1846, while repairing to Grind a

sithe on a stone attach'd to the Gear-
ing in the Woollen Factory. He was
entangled. His death was sudden and
awful.

Children fared little better than their watchful elders when
it came to accidental passings. Certainly, as is proven by the great
number of tombstones marking the graves of youngsters, a child
was really quite fortunate to survive to adulthood. In Newport,
Rhode Island, we find sad evidence of this type of hardship suf-
fered by William and Sarah Langley, who buried six children in a
single grave.

Other epitaphs found throughout New England speak of
the untimely demise of youngsters in graphic detail: of the young
boy who "fell in a cistern"; of a five-year old who "slipped through
the ice"; and of twins who were "charred by fire." Perhaps one
verse said it all when it stated:

> From Death's arrest no
> age is free.
> Young children too may die.

Mothers often died along with their offspring during child-
birth, with many being buried side-by-side. "Childbed fever," as it
was known, took a huge toll on the population, as did a number of
other ailments. "Consumption" seems to have been one of the
major culprits, while others were "removed by dysentery." A man
who lived in 18th century Massachusetts "died of a bellyache"
while, not far away, a young lady who was "on a journey in pursuit
of health, died suddenly of a violent Hectick Complaint."

A great deal of the humor discovered on headstones by
contemporary researchers and collectors was unintentional.
Misspellings, misuse of the English language, and misunderstood
passages seem to be the most common cause for our amusement.
The epitaph marking the grave of Marcy Halle, in Glastonbury,
Connecticut, is a prime example of this type of comedy of errors:

> Here lies one who
> os lifes thrads
> Cut a sunder She
> was strucke dead
> by a clap of thundr

Poor spelling and poor grammar make another epitaph, in the
Methodist Cemetery, St. Louis, Missouri, quite difficult to read:

Here lize a stranger braiv,
Who died while fightin' the Suthern
Confederacy to save
Piece to his dust.
Braive Suthern fiend
From iland 10
You reach a Glory us end.
We plase these flowrs above the
stranger's hed,
In honor of the shiverlus ded.
Sweet spirit rest in Heven
Ther'll be known Yankis there.

If you spend enough time in American graveyards, you will eventually be able to piece together large portions of forgotten history. Famous and infamous people alike will be remembered for their important contributions. Perhaps one of the most misunderstood men of his time was Thomas Paine, writer of *Common Sense*, who died in 1809. By that time he had been convicted of treason in Great Britain, imprisoned in France, denied citizenship in America, and forbidden burial in a Quaker churchyard. He died, poor and sick, in a New York City boarding house, and the only newspaper to mention his passing wrote the following intended tombstone inscription:

He had lived long,
done some good,
and much harm.

Paine's body was later exhumed, taken to England by William Cobbett, inhereted by Cobbett's son in 1835, seized by the Lord Chancellor when the son became bankrupt, and finally disappeared, lost to history for all time.

The circumstances that surrounded the death of Edgar Allen Poe seemed suspicious, to say the least. He was found in a semi-conscious state of mind outside of a Baltimore, Maryland, polling place. From there he was taken to a nearby hospital, where he died on Sunday, October 7, 1849. It was an election day, and most modern day historians believe that he was given an overdose of drugs and forced to vote several times. His tombstone sadly laments:

Quoth the Raven nevermore.

If historical accounts are to be believed, Meriwether Lewis - former leader of the Lewis and Clark expedition and the governor of the Louisiana territory - placed a gun to his head at a trailside inn in the desolate and savage Tennessee wilderness in the middle of the night and pulled the trigger. Next, or so the hard-to-believe story goes, he cried out "O Lord!", aimed again and shot himself in the stomach. After that, he had enough energy to crawl almost helplessly to the innkeeper's door, where he begged for help, but was refused. In great pain, he crawled back to his sleeping quarters and aimlessly hacked at his own, weakened body with a hunting knife. Finally, after laying in his own blood for several hours, he expired.

Lewis had no money in his possession when authorities arrived on the scene. Within a few weeks thereafter, the innkeeper who had refused to offer assistance, suddenly came into a mysterious fortune, moved to another town, and purchased a prime chunk of land. Furthermore, Lewis's halfbreed servant, to whom he owed money, disappeared without a trace; his watch turned up later in New Orleans.

Despite the strange circumstances surrounding Lewis's death, it was ruled that he had committed suicide. Yet, how are we to even begin to believe that this veteran combat soldier and rugged frontiersman, vastly experienced in the use of all types of weapons, had so completely and utterly screwed up the job? In any case, he was buried where he had died, and his grave remained unmarked for nearly forty years. Today, an unsightly, cracked shaft of cement, vacant of an epitaph, marks his tomb; a fitting monument, perhaps, to his mysterious death.

Chang and Eng Bunker were notorious for being totally compatible. They were literally forced to be so by a thin, muscular connection which bound them together below the chest. Known as the original "Siamese Twins," the story of their death should be as unforgettable as their lives.

After having been the highlight of P.T. Barnum's circus, the two retired to Mount Airy, North Carolina, where they planned to live out their lives in obscurity. After buying a farm, they married sisters, and settled down to raise a joint family of nineteen children. As time went by, however, the two sisters became tired of one another. There was only one solution to their predicament: they set up separate households and every three days, without fail, Chang and Eng would move a mile and a half down the road to accomodate the feuding wives.

One cold and blustery January evening, after having made the journey, Chang talked his brother into sitting next to a warm fire to get rid of his chill. Two days later, Eng awoke to discover that his brother had died. Terrified, he began to shake uncontrollably, which was followed by a choking sensation. Within two hours, Eng also expired. Doctors later determined that Chang had died from pneumonia, while Eng had died of fright. The brothers had a double funeral, and were buried in a double coffin beneath a double tombstone.

Thirty miles from where Abraham Lincoln lies entombed, in Oakland Cemetery, Petersburg, Illinois, is the grave of Ann Rutledge. Her name has repeatedly been linked to that of the sixteenth president in both scandalous fact and fiction. According to some, had she not died of malaria at the age of 22, she would have been the first lady. Her epitaph further makes this claim:

> I am Ann Rutledge who sleep beneath
> these weeds,
> Beloved of Abraham Lincoln,
> Wedded to him, not through union,
> But through separation.

Though Patrick Henry, Revolutionary instigator, statesman, and speaker, should be remembered for a great many things, his epitaph sums it up in only five words:

> His fame his best epitaph.

Although no marker adorns the Baltimore grave of John Wilkes Booth, the actor did not go without a tribute. A Confederate veteran placed the following in front of his home in Troy, Alabama:

> Erected by Pink Parker
> in honor of John Wilkes Booth
> for killing old Abe Lincoln.

Parker asked that the stone be placed over his own grave. The request was carried out, but only after the inscription was replaced with a more conventional epitaph.

Eugene Gladstone O'Neill, playwright and author of *Long Day's Journey Into Night*, wrote parallels to his tragic life. He died in Boston Hotel room in 1953, and was laid to rest in the Forest Hills Cemetery, Jamaica Plain, Massachusetts. Though there is no epitaph adorning his tombstone, executors might have inscibed his final words:

I knew it, I knew it!
Born in a goddam hotel room and dying in a hotel
room!

By the time that Emily Dickinson died on May 15, 1886, she had lived most of her life in total seclusion. During those years, no one but the immediate family was allowed to see her unless they stood out in a darkened hall. Her stone, in West Cemetery, Amherst, Massachusetts, reads simply:

Called back.

John A. Joyce, poet, wrote a punning epitaph for himself:

Spread golden flowers upon my life,
And do so very often -
I need them in my daily life
But not upon my coffin.

James Butler Hickok, better known as "Wild Bill," will always be remembered for his death in Deadwood, South Dakota. As he sat playing poker, holding a pair of aces and eights, he was shot in the back of the head. His tombstone reads:

Pard, we will meet again in the happy
hunting ground to part no more.
Colorado Charlie

Twenty-seven years later, Martha Jane Cannary Burke (Calamity Jane) had become a hopeless alcoholic. Before she died, she said:

Bury me next to Bill

That's exactly what the good folks of Deadwood did.

Lydia Estes Pinkham, inventor of Pinkham's Vegetable Compound, died in 1883. Though few may remember her today, her name was a household word during the 19th century. She is also credited with writing the first widely read sex manual. Though it isn't on her headstone, a little poem made popular more than 100 years ago would be quite appropriate:

Oh we sing of Lydia Pinkham
And her love for the human race.
She invented the Vegetable Compound
And the label bears her face.

45

Poet Robert Frost, who is buried in the First Congregational Church Cemetery, Old Bennington, Vermont, led a tragic life. He had two sons who died young; a daughter who died while giving birth; and a wife who died of a heart attack after 40 years of marriage. Reportedly, he felt bitter toward his tragic luck, for his epitaph so prophetically said:

I had a lover's quarrel with the world.

Carrie Amelia Nation, famous saloon smasher in the early 1900's, is laid to rest in Belton Cemetery, Belten, Missouri. While she was still alive, New York bars sported signs that read "Welcome all Nations but Carry." She died in 1911, before alcohol was officially outlawed, and, exasperatingly, her epitaph reads:

She hath done what she could

Though journalist Henry Louis Mencken has no epitaph upon his tomb, he had, indeed, composed one before he died:

If after I depart this vale, you ever
remember me and have thought to please
my ghost, forgive some sinner and wink
your eye at some homely girl.

Many people believe that the tombstone of accused axe murderer Lizzie Andrew Borden should read:

Lizzie Borden took an axe
And gave her mother forty wacks;
And when that job was nicely done,
She gave her father forty-one.

Upon close inspection, the arrangement of the three tombstones (her father's, mother's, and her own) seems a bit hideous. Her parents were buried in a decapitated state, and when Lizzie was buried 35 years later, she was laid to rest nearby. Andrew and Abby form the base of a triangle--or the feet--and Lizzie the apex--or the head. What most people don't know is that Lizzie was acquitted of the brutal crime.

Thus ends a brief collection of epitaphs, which I have gathered during my many years of searching painstakingly through cemeteries and burial grounds all across America. Deleted are hundreds of others, which speak of those "killed by doctors"; a youngster "by boiling cyder she was slain"; a boy who was "kicked in the head by a mule"; and a soldier killed "by the accidental discharge of a cannon."

As you begin your collection, keep in mind that not all inscriptions speak the truth. Some are mistake-ridden, misleading, or misinterpreted. One, found over a woman from Skaneateles, New York, was purposely incorrect; not to protect the innocent, but to bring it into correct verse:

> Underneath this pile of stones
> Lies all that's left of Sally Jones.
> Her name was Lord, it was not Jones,
> But Jones was used to rhyme with stones.

Sermons in stone were not meant to be unquestionable historical fact. Instead, they were designed and carved as a general reminder of the past. Therefore, we should take them at simple face value, for they offer us a broad portrait of God-fearing, strong-willed people who lived their lives according to the best of their abilities. That alone is their claim to fame.

At the age of twenty-three, while a journeyman printer, Benjamin Franklin wrote for himself the following epitaph, which might be dedicated to all Americans, past and present:

> Like the cover of an old book,
> its contents torn out
> and stripped of its lettering and gilding,
> lies here, food for worms.
> But the work shall not be wholly lost;
> for it will, as he believed, appear
> once more,
> in a new and more perfect addition
> corrected and amended
> by the Author.

Chapter 5

How To Locate A Particular Ancestor's Grave

Life is a jest, and all things show it:
I thought so once, but now I know it.

If you are a collector of tombstone memorabilia who is just beginning to embark on the task of locating a particular relative in a specific cemetery or graveyard, you would do well to first recall an amusing moral parallel. One fine autumn day, while out harvesting apples from his orchard, a farmer came upon the most amazing specimen he had ever laid eyes upon: an apple that was immaculately ripened to a deep red, and almost bursting with nature's juices. The farmer snatched the apple from the branch, strolled gallantly into his barn, and climbed high up into the hay loft. Certainly, he thought, this near-perfect apple should be joyously consumed by the grower, and he prepared himself to commence eating.

However, as his jaws separated for that first delicious bite, the apple slipped from his hand and dropped into the large hay-stack below. Quickly the farmer jumped down from the loft and desperately began searching for the apple. His hands sifted through the hay, stalk by stalk, slowly turning his fingers chafed and raw. Despite his efforts, however, the apple could not be found. After many intense hours of relentless searching, he surrendered in exhausted despair. Standing upright and brushing the clinging hay from his body, he realized that his efforts had been "fruitless", and he stomped out of the dusty barn. Moments later, the farmer's aging and crippled horse stepped directly to just the right spot, stuck his nose deep into the hay, and came up clenching the lost apple in his teeth. Soon the wonderful fruit was completely devoured.

The meaning of the story is quite simple: a thing is only lost until the ideal searcher or search methods are employed to locate it. Keep this in mind as you begin your investigation for the buried remains of your ancestors. Such an endeavor will quite possibly escort you down avenues of historical research that are relatively unknown, infrequently traveled, and therefore extremely difficult to follow. The entire process can be overwhelming to the average freelance tombstone researcher, unless he or she knows precisely how to go about conducting a step-by-step investigation. However, searching for a specific grave marker in a specific graveyard is much different than looking for an apple in a haystack: the apple is without a doubt much easier to find.

I am most certainly not trying to discourage you from your research efforts; nor am I claiming that using aging burial grounds to your genealogical advantage is a next to impossible task. Rather, I am simply offering you fair warning that cemetery research will pose some unique difficulties which have, until now, limited our use of them.

In a number of ways, tombstone inscriptions are a great deal like vital records collections or the national census. They offer us much of the same data and information, including birth, death, and marriage records. What we might ordinarily uncover on paper or microfilm, however, is deeply etched into stone, and can survive a good deal longer than written statistics, assuming that the grave marker is still intact.

Generally speaking, there are five different types of burial sites in America, the most prevalent of which is the government-owned and operated cemetery. Such a graveyard can be controlled by the township, city, county, state, or national government. This controlling agency writes all rules and regulations pertaining to the burial site, including everything from what size and shape of markers are allowed to the banning of inground plants and shrubs. Since such cemeteries are normally supported financially by the taxpayers, it is the citizenry that has the final say over rules and regulations governing the site.

A second type of burial ground is called a church yard, which is simply a piece of land adjacent to a church which has been converted to a cemetery. This custom for interment was imported from England, and is most common within early colonial states. Under normal circumstances, only church members were allowed burial within this type of confine.

The third type of burial site is also under the control of a specific church; however, the land is not immediately adjacent to the church structure itself, but rather separately located some distance away. Known as a church-owned graveyard, it is somewhat distinct from the church yard in that outside members were sometimes allowed burial within its boundaries. Most often this included the prominent and well-to-do members of the community, as well as those living elsewhere who were related to a family which could claim membership within the church.

The fourth type of burial site is the privately-owned cemetery, which is typically controlled by a corporate structure and is operated in a business-like fashion. Here, rules and regulations are set down by the corporate members and the site is paid for out of membership fees and plot purchases. Though the ordinary epitaph researcher may be somewhat unfamiliar with such an arrangement, there are a great many cemeteries of this type scattered throughout the United States. Perhaps the vague knowledge of their existence comes from the fact that they were more recently established, and not many epitaphs are found therein.

Finally, we in America and throughout the rest of the world have created burial sites known as the family graveyard. Typically located in a small, out-of-the-way corner of a family farm or estate, they are often left unkempt. Hence, bushes, trees, and tall grasses shroud their existence which in turn makes them difficult to locate. Though each of the five types of graveyards outlined can present problems that are unique, the family graveyard is by far the most difficult to deal with.

Before embarking on your trek to locate your buried ancestors or forefathers, you must first determine the general region of burial. Hence, your task begins much like a writer attempting to turn a 5,000 word essay into one that possesses a mere 100 words.

If, however, the person you are seeking was buried in a rather large community like Chicago or Boston, the problem is one of expansion, for there will be a number of cemeteries in which to search. My best advice would be to start by locating a "road map" of sorts, which may simply be an obituary or death certificate. Yet, please be further advised that these too have their limitations, especially if the death occurred more than a century ago. Instead, other vital statistics, such as birth, baptismal, and marriage records can put you on the right track; hence that is where your search should begin.

The American system of maintaining vital records is, quite literally, unique when we compare it to systems used in other countries, even though its basic foundation was set forth in Great Britain. Beginning in 1538, following the emancipation of the Church of England from the Roman Catholic Church, it was ordered that ministers were to keep an accurate, up to-date record of baptisms, marriages, and burials within the pages of individual parish registers. Since this was nearly three-quarters of a century before the first permanent British colony in America, you might think that such a law would solve all of your problems. Indeed, it might have if the law had been strictly adhered to; but it was not.

The first known similar statute in America was passed by Virginia's Grand Assembly in 1632. This regulation dictated that the "minister or warden of each parish appear in court once a year on the first day of June and present a record of christenings, marriages and burials for the preceding year." Though few people thought much of it at the time, these records initiated the move toward maintaining accurate vital statistics, including records of births, marriages, and deaths.

Just seven years later, in 1639, the General Court of the Massachusetts Bay Colony required township clerks to record actual births and deaths, rather than christenings and burials. Thus, we see a method of pinpointing these valuable vital statistics to the day of occurrence. Furthermore the law also removed the burden of record-keeping from individual parishes and placed it in the hands of government officials. Soon thereafter, Connecticut, Old Colony (Plymouth), and other colonies would follow the lead put forth by Massachusetts.

As time passed, legal jurisdictions mandated the collection, maintenance, and preservation of these records. Early laws were updated and reinforced by new laws, with the Massachusetts Bay Colony once again leading the way. In 1644, that colony added a penalty for those who failed to report accurate vital events. Eventually, in 1692, the colony went as far as to establish a registration fee amounting to three pence for each birth and death that occurred. Furthermore, a stiffer fine was initiated for those who failed to report such events. And, to top it off, the act allowed township clerks the right to issue birth and death certificates as proof of such vital statistics!

None of these early statutes proved very effective for the later genealogical researcher. For decades to come, problems pervaded the system, especially since coverage was incomplete. Indeed, townships and cities had governing ordinances, but there was not an entire state that possessed complete registration laws until the mid-1800's. Furthermore, the incoming population was so transient that such laws were difficult to enforce. Simply put, failure to obey these regulations was just another method used by mobile Americans to rebel against higher government taxes and fees.

Historically speaking, therefore, American citizens needed a much stronger reason than monetary penalties to comply with the law. And that better reason was given to them by an unexpected source - the medical profession. Physicians, and those who maintained medical statistics, had come up with the concept that it was of utmost importance to know not merely the number of deaths, but the causes of death as well. Only then would it be possible to fight deadly disease and control epidemics. Writing of this development in Great Britain in a booklet entitled "Evolution of Preventive Medicine," Sir Arthur Newsholme stated:

> Panic was a large part in securing repentance and good works when cholera threatened; as it, likewise, was in an earlier century when plague became epidemic; and in both instances the desire for complete and accurate information as to the extent of the invasion led England to the call for accurate vital statistics. It may truly be said that the early adoption of accurate registers of births and deaths was hastened by fears of cholera...

Within the U.S., statistics of vital interest have never been maintained at the national level, as they have been in other countries. Instead, such responsibilities were handed over to the individual states. Hence, each of our fifty states has developed its own system of recording deaths and burials.

For the epitaph collector, such records can prove invaluable, particularly if he or she is attempting to locate the burial site of a specific relative. Well, you will be happy to hear that an extensive directory to such information was compiled within many states during the late 1930's and early 1940's by the Works Projects Administration as part of its Historical Records Survey. No less than forty states participated in the immense project, excluding Alaska (not yet a state), Connecticut, Deleware, Hawaii (not yet a state), Maine, Maryland, Ohio, Pennsylvania, South Carolina, and Vermont.

Each state that did participate subsequently published a guide to vital statistics records available by county, city, and township within its own boundaries. Copies of these collections are available through numerous large public and university libraries, as well as historical societies. The list, alphabetized by state, pertinent to epitaph collectors (with supplimentary information added for missing states) is as follows:

Alabama: "Guide to Public Vital Statistics Records in Alabama: Preliminary Edition," March, 1942. "Guide to Vital Statistics Records in Alabama: Church Archives," May, 1942.

Alaska: No booklets available. Death records are available since 1913 from the Bureau of Vital Statistics, Department of Health and Social Services, Pouch H-02G, Juneau, Alaska, 99811.

Arizona: "Guide to Public Vital Statistics Records in Arizona," August, 1942.

Arkansas: No booklets available. Death records are available since February of 1914 from the Division of Vital Records, Arkansas Department of Health, Little Rock, Arkansas, 72201.

California: "Guide to Public Vital Statistics Records in California," Vol. II, Death Records, July, 1941. "Guide to Church Vital Records in California: Alameda and San Francisco Counties; Six Denominations," May, 1942.

Colorado: "Guide to Vital Statistics Records in Colorado," Vol. I, Public Archives, 1942; Vol. II, Church Archives, 1942.

Connecticut: "The Barbour Collection," (vital records compiled from church, cemetery and town records before 1850). "The Hale Collection," (marriages, deaths and burials from cemetery inscriptions and newspapers: pre-Civil War).

Delaware: Death records, 1855-1910 (with a card index available from "very early" to 1888), the Hall of Records, Dover, Delaware.

District of Columbia: No booklets available. Death records are available since 1855 from the Vital Records Section, Room 1028, 300 Indiana Avenue N.W., Washington, DC, 20001.

Florida: "Guide to Public Vital Statistics Records in Florida," February, 1941. "Guide to Supplementary Vital Statistics Records in Florida: Preliminary Edition." Vol. I, Aluchu, June, 1942; Vol. II, Gilchrist, June, 1942: Vol. III, Orange, June, 1942.

Georgia: "Guide to Public Vital Statistics Records in Georgia," June, 1941.

Hawaii: No booklets available. A scattering of death records are available from the Research and Statistics Office, State Department of Health, P.O. Box 3378, Honolulu, Hawaii, 96801.

Idaho: Guide to Public Vital Statistics Records in Idaho: State and County," March, 1942.

Illinois: "Guide to Public Vital Statistics Records in Illinois," May, 1941.

Indiana: "Guide to Public Vital Statistics Records in Indiana," July, 1941.

Iowa: Guide to Public Vital Statistics Records in Iowa," October, 1941.

Kansas: Guide to Public Vital Statistics Records in Kansas," March, 1942.

Kentucky: Guide to Public Vital Statistics Records in Kentucky," February, 1942.

Louisiana: "Guide to Public Vital Statistics Records in Louisiana," December, 1942. "Guide to Vital Statistics Records in Church Archives in Louisiana," Vol. I, Protestant and Jewish Church, December, 1942: Vol. II, Roman Catholic Church, December, 1942.

Maine: Vital records index, early to 1892. These records are incomplete, at best. They can be secured from approximately 80 townships by contacting individual town clerks in the town where the death occurred. A total of 17 township records have been published by the Maine Historical Society.

Maryland: Indexes in the Hall of Records, Annapolis, Maryland, for deaths, 1865-1880, for Anne Arundel County, and a few in the 1600's for Charles, Kent, Somerset, and Talbot counties.

Massachusetts: "Guide to Public Vital Statistics Records in Massachusetts," 1942. Church and cemetery records have also been published for more than 200 townships throughout the state by the New England Historic Genealogical Society, Franklin P. Rice, and the Essex Institute.

Michigan: "Vital Statistics Holdings by Government Agencies in Michigan," Death Records, July, 1942. "Guide to Church Vital Statistics Records in Michigan: Wayne County," April, 1942.

Minnesota: "Guide to Public Vital Statistics Records in Minnesota," 1941. "Guide to Church Vital Statistics Records in Minnesota," April, 1942.

Mississippi: "Guide to Vital Statistics Records in Mississippi," Vol. I, Public Archives, April, 1942; Vol. II, Church Archives, July, 1942.

Missouri: "Guide to Public Vital Statistics Records in Missouri," July, 1941. "Guide to Vital Statistics: Church Records in Missouri," April, 1942.

Montana: "Guide to Public Vital Statistics Records in Montana," March, 1941. "Inventory of the Vital Statistics Records of Churches and Religious Organizations in Montana, Preliminary Edition," July, 1942.

Nebraska: "Guide to Public Vital Statistics Records in Nebraska," September, 1941.

Nevada: "Guide to Public Vital Statistics Records in Nevada," December, 1941.

New Hampshire: "Guide to Public Vital Statistics Records in New Hampshire," 1941. "Guide to Church Vital Statistics Records in New Hampshire, Preliminary Edition," May, 1942.

New Jersey: "Guide to Vital Statistics Records in New Jersey," Vol. I, Public Archives, 1942; Vol. II, Church Archives, 1942.

New Mexico: Guide to Public Vital Statistics Records in New Mexico," March, 1942.

New York: "Guide to Public Vital Statistics Records in New York State," Vol. III, Death Records, 1942. "Guide to Vital Statistics Records in Churches in New York State (Exclusive of New York City)." Vol. I, May, 1942; Vol. II, June, 1942. "Guide to Vital Statistics Records in the City of New York: Churches," Borough of Bronx, April, 1942; Borough of Brooklyn, 1942; Borough of Manhattan, 1942; Borough of Queens, May, 1942; Borough of Richmond, 1942.

North Carolina: "Guide to Vital Statistics Records in North Carolina," Vol. I, Public Vital Statistics, June, 1942.

North Dakota: "Guide to Public Vital Statistics Records of North Dakota," August, 1941. "Guide to Church Vital Statistics Records in North Dakota," March, 1942.

Ohio: No booklets available. Death records are available since December of 1908 from the Division of Vital Statistics, State Department of Health, G-20 State Departments Building, Columbus, Ohio, 43215. Prior to December of 1908, death records are available from local probate courts, located in the county where death occurred.

Oklahoma: "Guide to Public Vital Statistics Records in Oklahoma," June, 1941.

Oregon: "Guide to Public Vital Statistics Records in Oregon," April, 1942.

Pennsylvania: No booklets available. Death records are available since 1906 from the Division of Vital Statistics, P.O. Box 1528, New Castle, Pennsylvania, 16103. Prior to 1906, death records are available from the county where the event took place.

Rhode Island: "Guide to Public Vital Statistics Records: Births, Marriages, Deaths in the State of Rhode Island and Providence Plantations," June, 1941. "Summary of Legislation Concerning Vital Statistics in Rhode Island," July, 1937. "The Arnold Collection of Vital Records: 1636-1850," 21 volumes.

South Carolina: No booklets available. Death records are available from the Bureau of Vital Statistics, State Board of Health, Sims Building, Columbia, South Carolina, 29201.

South Dakota: "Guide to Public Vital Statistics Records in South Dakota," January, 1942.

Tennessee: "Guide to Public Vital Statistics Records in Tennessee," June, 1941. "Guide to Church Vital Statistics Records in Tennessee," August, 1942.

Texas: "Guide to Public Vital Statistics Records in Texas," June, 1941.

Utah: "Guide to Public Vital Statistics Records in Utah," November, 1941. "Census of Weber County (Exclusive of Green River Precinct), Provisional State of Deseret, 1850," October, 1937.

Vermont: An index to vital records exists from early through 1908 at the Secretary of State's Office, Montpelier, Vermont.

Virginia: "Guide to the Manuscript Collections of the Virginia Baptist Historical Society. Supplement No. 1, Index to the

Obituary Notices in the *Religious Herald*, Richmond, Virginia, 1828 - 1938," Vol. I, A-L, August, 1941, Vol. II, M-Z, September, 1941.

Washington: "Guide to Public Vital Statistics Records in Washington," June, 1941. "Guide to Church Vital Statistics Records in Washington. Preliminary Edition," February, 1942.

West Virginia: "Inventory of Public Vital Statistics Records in West Virginia: Births, Deaths, and Marriages," March, 1941. "Guide to Church Vital Statistics Records in West Virginia," February, 1942.

Wisconsin: "Guide to Public Vital Statistics Records in Wisconsin," September, 1941. "Guide to Church Vital Statistics Records in Wisconsin," September, 1941.

Wyoming: "Guide to Public Vital Statistics Records in Wyoming," June, 1941. "Guide to Vital Statistics Records in Wyoming: Church Archives, Preliminary Edition," March, 1941.

Once you have determined the most likely place of death for a specific ancestor, use the above list of booklets and information to secure a death certificate.

For your own future benefit as a genealogist and ancestral epitaph collector, you would be well off to secure a pamphlet, entitled *Where to Write for Birth and Death Records*. Compiled by the National Office of Vital Statistics, Public Health Service, United States Department of Health, Education, and Welfare, it covers all states and territories controlled by the United States. It is available, for a minimal fee, by simply writing to:

> Superintendent of Documents
> United States Government Printing Office
> Washington, D.C. 20402

When writing for copies of death certificates and records it is best to keep your inquiry as brief as possible. Not only will township clerks and genealogical record keepers avoid reading lengthy letters, but your request may be totally lost within the body of your inquiry. It is also advisable to disclose your relationship to the deceased, since a number of vital statistics offices refuse to supply records to non-relatives. And, finally, you should send the exact amount of money needed for processing along with your request. Cashier's checks and money orders are appropriate, rather than personal checks, if you desire quick results.

When asking for a copy of a person's death certificate, you will save yourself a good deal of time by supplying all information you know about the event. The following is an example of a death certificate request letter, although adjustments must be made to fit specific inquiries:

P.O. Box 599

Winn, MI 48896

Office of Vital Records
P.O. Box 60630
New Orleans, Louisiana 70160

August 19, 1990

To Whom It May Concern:

I would appreciate it if you would send me a copy of the death certificate of my great grandfather, George Peter Johnson, who died July 23, 1832, in New Orleans, at the age of 88. His father was Joseph Stephen Johnson and his wife was Matilda Johnson.

Enclosed you will find a money order in the amount of three dollars ($3.00) to cover your fee. Thank you very much for your valuable time and consideration concerning this matter.

Sincerely,

(signed) Thomas W. Johnson

Most importantly, the date of death is needed, since most records are maintained chronologically. The place of death is not always needed, though the specific full name of the individual is absolutely essential.

After you have determined the place of your ancestor's death, you may want to check local obituary notices if available. This will offer some assistance in pinpointing the specific cemetery in which he or she was buried.

Simply knowing the name of the cemetery in question does not mark the end of your quest, however, for your problems are most assuredly not over. Although larger cemeteries are usually listed in the local telephone directory, smaller ones are not. Don't give up hope, however, for it is not beyond the realm of reality to cross a specific "location" hurdle. In fact, there are three possible sources to investigate.

First, check with local chambers of commerce, city halls, or governmental agencies. They should be able to direct you to a specific cemetery's location. However, if this should fail, try purchasing U.S. Government Geological Survey maps of the region, which are detailed enough to show even the smallest of graveyards. Finally, ask local residents in the general vicinity: much of the time, they can provide information and direction when all other avenues have turned into dead ends.

The next logical step once you have found the burial site is to check out any available sexton's records. Once again, this job can be quite problematic. Family-owned cemeteries will have no sexton's records whatsoever; in reality, count yourself extremely fortunate if you even find intact tombstones within these often neglected burial sites.

On the other hand, church yards seldom keep specific records, other than possible information concerning who once owned the various plots. Those cemeteries owned and operated by private and government agencies, however, normally keep accurate, up-to-date records concerning lot ownership and, sometimes, burial location. Still other grave yards possess extensive information on everyone buried there, though you won't know until you investigate the matter. Despite the often vague data, such records can save you a good deal of time and energy that you might instead expend wandering around within a massive graveyard.

Keep in mind while thumbing through church registers and sexton's records that you will encounter a number of different ways of indexing particular information. I have found every system imaginable, from numerical arrangement by lot number (which has absolutely nothing to do with names or purchase dates) to alphabetical order by maiden name.

If you are the sort of researcher who does not wish to travel cross-country in order to seek out long-lost ancestors, perhaps the nearest university library can be of some assistance. Many possess collections of epitaphs that have been methodically copied down by researchers, and then transferred to microfilm. The organizations responsible for copying such collections include: the Daughters of the American Revolution (DAR), which transcribed inscriptions from thousands of cemeteries throughout the country;

the Works Projects Administration (WPA), which undertook a similar project during the Great Depression; the Daughters of the Utah Pioneers; and the Idaho Genealogical Society. These groups, and many others, may have unwittingly provided you with an avenue to your own roots which will not demand a great deal of exhausting effort on your part. Check the indexes of their research.

Looking for long-lost relatives in burial sites throughout the country can, indeed, be a painstaking process. Yet with a bit of patience you will be successful in your attempt. If not, do not despair - you will most likely come across some interesting epitaphs that you will want to save solely for the sake of posterity.

Chapter 6

Deciphering Epitaphs

Here lies Inter'd ye Remains of ye
Refpectable Elisha Lyon Eldeft Son of
Capt. Nehemiah Lyon & Mehetable his
wife. He died Oct. 15th 1767 in ye 24th
year of His Age. His Death is mournfully
memorable, on account of the manner and
Occafion. For as He was Decently going
thro' the military manual Exercife. in the
Company under Comand of Capt. Elisha
Child. Sd Capt. Giving ye words of
Command. He was Wounded by ye
difcharge of Fire arms ufed by one of
ye Company. Sd arms having been
Loaded Intirely unknown to him,
ye wound was Inftantaneous Death.

One job of the epitaph collector is to read, decipher, and translate words. Therefore, it naturally follows that, in order for you to be a well-versed interpreter, you must be familiar with the basic foundation of the inscribed language. Furthermore, since it is virtually impossible to know every nation's variations of vocabulary, dialect, and street jargon, you may need to locate a knowledgable source for accurate interpretation. This, by the way, is not always possible: a single language, such as Spanish, may have more than a hundred dialect variations, depending on precise region of origin. For the specific purpose of reading and understanding American epitaphs, however, we will concentrate on English.

I have a college friend who came to America from West Germany, so whenever I encounter a German term that I do not comprehend, I call upon her to interpret. More often than not, however, the term is not familiar to her, even though she was born, raised, and educated in that country. The first time that she was noticeably baffled by her native tongue, I was literally shocked. How could someone born in Germany not comprehend her own language?

As I became more involved with the study and interpretation of epitaphs, however, I gradually came to understand the answer: it wasn't a problem of not knowing German, but rather one of not having a full comprehension of all German jargons. Similarly, I might ask an American off the street to interpret the term "rad" and he or she may have no idea what it means. This, too, is the problem when an epitaph collector attempts to interpret the English language that was popular during the 17th, 18th, and 19th centuries: usage, spellings, and unfamiliar words must be understood. Hence, in this chapter I will try to bridge the gap between the past and present, so that the researcher may come to recognize some of the more common problem-terms.

The vast majority of collectors will need a basic foundation in the ability to recognize writing styles. Initially, you may wonder why style is discussed in a how-to book on epitaph collecting. After all, aren't most American styles recent enough that they are not that different from years past? The simple answer is no. In all actuality, the styles have sufficiently evolved, particularly since the colonial period, that a brief lesson is in order.

Even in our own time, many of us write or print in such a way that others cannot read it without a great deal of effort. At times, a few select individuals are even unable to read their own written words. And, if your direct ancestors were living in New England or along the Atlantic coast during the 1600's and 1700's, you will find a strange type of style on their headstones.

More than likely, the unfamiliar terms were carried over into America from an alphabet known as Middle English. Therefore, if you are truly serious about interpreting what you find etched in stone from this time period, a study of the simpler Middle English terms and alphabets will prove extremely useful. I suggest that you go to your local library and find a book that was co-authured by David E. Gardner and Frank Smith, and first published by Bookcraft in 1964, entitled *Genealogical Research in England and Wales*, Vol. III (Salt Lake City). It will undoubtedly help you become more adept at interpreting early tombstone inscriptions.

Despite your efforts, however, you may discover that a number of colonial epitaphs were not printed in English at all, but in some other European language. However, this is an extensive problem that cannot easily be tackled in a single chapter on interpreting epitaphs. Therefore, it will not be discussed here. Your best bet when you encounter the problem of breaking the language barrier would be to seek the help of an expert.

Often, when I am hard at work cleaning a headstone in preparation for a photograph or a rubbing, I discover that the inscribed words are impossible to interpret. For a time, I was fully convinced that the major qualification for becoming a stone cutter in early America was to be able to print so that no one else could read your words. Since that time, however, I have come to understand that most stone cutters took extreme care in their writing prowess and that most passages are indeed readable. Hence, the difficulty was not with the writer, but rather with the reader. In fact, much of the early American language can be interpreted quite easily if you familiarize yourself with a few common writing practices.

Perhaps the most easily misunderstood and therefore unappreciated practice from past generations is the art of abbreviation. This custom, used extensively on headstones throughout America, originated from the art of abbreviating in Latin, which was the official formal language used on early grave markers in England. Eventually, a British law was passed in 1733, forbidding the use of Latin in church registers. Yet, the same did not hold true for headstones, and a good deal of Latin and extensive use of abbreviated Latin terms continued after that time. This, in turn, was imported to America, with abbreviation habits applied to the English language.

Most abbreviations are quite readily recognized and understood if you remember that the majority of early tombstone carvers incorporated them in their work. However, until the 20th century, very few of what we call standard abbreviations had been established. Therefore, most words were shortened in a number of different ways. Still, the following list will offer a bit of insight into the problem:

according - accordg
account - accompt, accot, acct
administration - adminion, admon
administrator - adminr
aforesaid - aforsd, forsd, afors:, afsd.
and - &
and so forth - &c, etc. (etcetera)
can - cn, gin, gn
captain - captn, capt:
church - chh
daughter - dau, daur, dautr
deceased - decd

ditto - do
Doctor - Doc, Docr, Doctr
Esquire - Esq:, Esqr, Esq.
executor - execr, exr, exor
gentleman - gentln, gent:, gent.
honorable - honble, hon:
interred - intrd, interd, inter'd
Junior - Junr, Jr, Jun
Messieurs - Messrs, Mess
namely - viz, viz:, vizt (videlicet)
paid - pd
pair - pr
per - pr
personal - personl, p'sonl
received - recd, recvd
receipt - rect
record - recd
register - regr, registr
said - sd
Senior - Senr, Sr, Sen
testament - testamt, testa
the - ye
year - yr

A typical example of the use of abbreviations can be seen in the epitaph of Joseph Dudley, who was buried in England in 1510:

> Here is Mr Dudley Sen, & Jane his wife also;
> Who while livng was his super., but see what
> death gin do.
> To of his suns also lye here, one Walter,
> t'othr Junr;
> Yey all of yem went - in ye yr 1510 - b'low.

While studying tombstones, you will notice that many abbreviations were formulated by simply shortening the word. Furthermore, you may find that the final letter (or even the last two or three letters) at the end of the shortened form have been raised to a slightly higher level. This is known as superior letter abbreviation. In fact, on a number of occasions, I have discovered the term "Jr" with the "r" directly above the "J" in piggy-back fashion. Typically, this was done so that the reader would quickly be able to recognize the abbreviated form of the word. The same holds true for many of the shortened versions listed above.

Furthermore, it is essential to understand that words beginning with "th" were often printed on stones with a "y"; thus, "the" becomes "ye" and, similarly, "then" becomes "yen." This usage was quite common during the early days of America, and was simply a carry-over from the ancient Anglo-Saxon lettering. Other words beginning with "y" that should be pronounced with a "th" sound include "yere" and "yis."

Another often used abbreviation technique is "termination," which means quite simply cutting a word short and placing a period (.) or colon (:) after it (as in the case of "super.," which translates to "superior"). Termination of a word is also sometimes executed by simply etching a line (--) through the shortened version. Finally, in very early tombstone inscriptions only the first letter of some words was used.

You will also notice a third way to abbreviate words in the above epitaph: "contraction." The word "below," for example, has been contracted to "b'low." Furthermore, incorporating the same method, the two-word phrase of "the other" has been shortened by printing "t'othr." In these examples, an apostrophe (') is used, but I have also seen contractions created by placing a curved line immediately above the shortened word. You may also find words spelled with a double consonant written with only a single consonant and a straight line (---) drawn over it, signifying that it should contain two letters in succession. In colonial times, this was most often done with the letters "m" and "n", and the line was sometimes curved. During your investigation of tombstone literature you may find any number of words abbreviated in several different ways. In some instances, the same passage may in fact contain two totally different versions of the same word. And in other cases, two different words may have been shortened to the exact same abbreviation. In situations such as these, you should be able to recognize the meaning by simply reading the word in context.

Given names are often abbreviated on grave markers in much the same way as other words. However, be advised that there are exceptions to the rules. The following list of commonly shortened popular names will give you an idea of what you may find:

Aaron - Aarn
Abraham - Abram
Andrew - Andrw, Andw
Arthur - Artr, Arthr
Barbara - Barba
Benjamin - Benja, Benjn, Benj:
Charles - Chas, Chars

Christopher - Xr, Xopher, Xofer
Daniel - Danl
David - Davd
Ebenezer - Ebenr
Elizabeth - Eliza
Franklin - Frankln, Frankn, Frank
Frederick - Fredck, Fredrk
George - Geo:, Go
Gilbert - Gilbt, Gilrt
Hannah - Hanh
James - Jas
Jeremiah - Jera, Jerema, Jer:
Jonathan - Jonathn, Jonn, Jon:
John - Jno
Joseph - Jos
Leonard - Leond
Margaret - Margt
Nathan - Nathn
Nathaniel - Nathl, Nathanl
Patrick - Patrk
Richard - Richd, Rich:
Robert - Robt, Rob:
Samuel - Saml, Sam:
Stephen - Stephn
Thomas - Thos, Tho:
Vincent - Vinct, Vincnt
Virginia - Virga, Virg:
Wilford - Wilfd, Wilf:
William - Willm, Wm, Will:
Zachariah - Zacha, Zachara, Zach:

Once again, you'll find that there is no set standard for abbreviating names, though most often the final letter is slightly raised in the shortened version. Also quite common was the process of ending a given name abruptly and inserting a colon (:).

Throughout America, names from the Bible have long been bestowed on children as a sign of their purity. In New England, however, and in other localities along the Atlantic coast, uncommon names denoting human characteristics were often used. Thus, we find such colorful female names as Faith, Hope, Charity, Pennance, Sympathy, Prudence, Mercy, and Constance, while male names included Quality, Comfort, Consider, and even Remember.

On still other grave markers, you may find names so uncommon that they will make you laugh aloud. In many cases these were not taken from the Bible at all, and include terms used in everyday life. The most memorable that I have run across include "E Pluribus Unum," "Two Bits," and "Six Toes" (which may or may not have been referring to the child's extra digits).

In a great many families, given names were passed on from one generation to the next. At times, therefore, fathers, sons, and nephews would all have the same first name. Thus, in large families spread out across vast regions, it became somewhat difficult to distinguish between relatives.

In my own German ancestry, I have discovered that more than one child within the same family unit was given the same first name. Normally this was done when the first child had died, or was the result of two different marriages, though this was not the case in my family. "Theresa Schusahl," for example, was the name bestowed upon two distict siblings living at the same time, one of which was born in Germany and the other of which was born in America. However, I later discovered that such naming practices were indeed rare, and that it usually occurred in families of German and Dutch descent.

While perusing gravestone literature you will undoubtedly come across what seems like a tendency to capitalize the first letter of a word for no apparent reason. The same is true for entire words within a passage, or even single letters within a word. You may notice, however, that names and nouns were capitalized more often than other words, though there was little consistency among inscribers. The explanation, though evasive, seems to point toward the fact that specific words were more important to the cutter and were therefore capitalized to catch the attention of the reader. However, in some instances there is absolutely no rhyme or reason to the process. An example of this random capitalization can be seen on the tombstone of Annie Smith:

Here lyeth the BOdy of Mrs. ANIIE SMITH,
WhO dePrated thiS Life OCtO the 28, in the
yeare 1701.
Shee LiVed a Maid And died aged 708.

Ordinarily, you will also find an irregular use of punctuation on grave markers. In some inscriptions, you may find an occasional comma or period, while at other times there will be no punctuation at all. One practice followed by a number of stone cutters during the 18th and 19th centuries was to place a dot to signify a pause; a dot at base level indicated a brief pause, while a dot between the words indicated a phrase separation. These dots usually took the place of all other punctuation.

Perhaps one of the most difficult problems to deal with as an epitaph reader is that many inscribed letters look almost exactly alike. The capital "I" and "J", for example, are extremely troublesome to distinguish, as are the "T" and "F". For those stone cutters who adhered to the Roman alphabet, "U's" and "V's" were signified by the same letter.

Once again, there is no specific rule concerning what I refer to as look-alike lettering. Much deciphering depends on the inscriber, for there are other frequent letters that are quite difficult to discern. The best solution is to study the lettering very carefully in order to make a distinction whenever you run into a problem. Initials in the place of entire names, however, can pose an unsolvable situation, unless, of course, you already know the given name of the deceased.

Small, or lower case, letters may also give you fits in interpretation. Curlicues on the letter below a specific line, as with the letters "y" and "g", can cause difficulty, especially if they happen to run into other letters. Another troublesome letter is the long "s" which may appear as either a "p" or an "f", or even a double "f" or "p" (depending on how it was used). Hence, when you observe an inscribed word that contains an "fs" where you believe there should be a double "s", you are correct in your assumption. Although this arrangement was seldom used at the beginning or ending of a word, it was almost always used as the first letter of a double "s". This usage can be found on tombstones through the mid- to late-1800's.

In early Middle English inscriptions, the small "e" was etched in such a way that it resembles the modern "o", and it can cause errors in deciphering when it goes undetected. Hence, epitaph readers and collectors should be aware of possible translation problems at all times, lest the abbreviated form of Senior (Sen) may be interpretted as the word "Son."

Typically, whenever a stone cutter found it necessary to divide a word after running out of room at the end of a line, he did not use a hyphen (-). Instead, he incorporated either an equals sign (=) or a colon (:), often at the beginning of a line where the last portion of the divided word was being continued. As mentioned earlier, colons were also used quite frequently in forming abbreviations and, although it may seem confusing, context interpretation will maintain a distinction between the two.

On a great many headstones, I have seen an abrupt end of one word at the end of a line, only to find the continued word on the next line. At other times, I have found an unfamiliar abbreviated form of the word with no continuation at all. This was done, I suspect, simply because there was no more room, as seems to have been the case in a rather punning epitaph in northern Virginia which reads:

Let her RIP

Numbers have also been known to cause problems for the typical epitaph collector, as was the case in my very first cemetery outing. While searching for the headstone of Casper Schafer, one of my great-great-grandfathers, I found that the sandstone marker was rather badly weathered and worn. My eyes told me that he had died on September 10, 1862, although previous records indicated that he came to America from Germany in 1881. After doing a careful chalk rubbing of the stone, I discovered my error: the "6" in "1862" was, in reality, a "9", which put his death thirty years later.

The reason for my mistake, however, was not in the reading, but rather the writing. Numbers inscribed one, two, and even three centuries ago were written differently than we write them today. Therefore, numbers and dates written in the Arabic form need careful consideration in order to ensure proper interpretation. Furthermore, some numbers may not look like numbers at all. A specific case in point was the number "8," which was often inscribed to lie flat on its side. Also, in some instances you may even find Roman numerals, which require a certain degree of familiarity on the part of the reader.

Numbers as they relate to the calendar can also create difficulties, which may be rather surprising to you unless you fully understand the historical transition from the Julian system to the Gregorian system. As mentioned in an earlier chapter, the change took place in 1752.

During the period when the Julian system was being used, countries where the Christian Church was popular had what we call an ecclesiastical calendar (dating back to 325 A.D.). Using this type of calendar, we find that New Year's Day fell on March 25th instead of January 1st. This was celebrated as the Feast of the Annunciation, commonly referred to as "Lady Day," which marked the visit of the Angel Gabriel to the Virgin Mary to inform her of her impending motherhood. Thus, conception began exactly nine months prior to December 25th, the day of Christ's birth.

To illustrate the problems caused by such a system in our minds, let us take a look at a series of chronological dates under each system:

Julian Calendar	Gregorian Calendar
November 1, 1744	January 13, 1744
December 7, 1744	February 3, 1744
January 13, 1744	March 22, 1744
February 3, 1744	November 1, 1744
March 22, 1744	December 7, 1744
March 28, 1745	March 28, 1745
April 14, 1745	April 14, 1745

Hence, suppose someone who was born on March 22, 1744 died on March 28, 1745, as in the list above. Using this scenario, our "Gregorian trained" minds logically decipher this to mean that that person was just over one year of age at the time of death. However, since the Julian Calendar was then in use (and the new year began on March 25), that person was in actuality only six days old at the time of death. Thus, the problem arises from the simple fact that it is ingrained in our minds that the year begins on January first, and we automatically position a series of events in the wrong order if we use the Gregorian system.

To solve this problem, we incorporate what has come to be known in genealogical circles a double-dating. In other words, whenever you stumble upon a tombstone date that falls between January 1 and March 24, prior to 1752, you should reflect the fact by noting both the outdated and modern calendar systems. Otherwise, you will be trimming or adding an entire year to a person's life.

While researching the tombs of your ancestors, you may encounter some Latin terms or phrases that are unfamiliar to you. Although they were not used extensively in America, a few appear as carry-overs from English-styled markers, and they are common enough that some knowledge of them will be beneficial. For example, consider the following terms which you may come across during your search:

Anno Domini (A.D.) - in the year of our Lord
circa (c., ca., circ.) - about
esse - is
et alii (et al .) - and others

etcetera (etc., &c) - and so forth
fugit hora - the hour is fleeting - also, likewise
mortalem - mortal
memento - recall, remember
memento mori - remember that you must die
nepos - grandson
obiit (ob) - he died, she died
requiescat in pace (R.I.P.) - may he/she rest in peace
sic - so, thus
te - that
testes - witnesses
ultimo (ult.) - last, final
uxor (us, vx) - wife
videlicet (viz, vizt) - namely

Thus, if you run across a common phrase, such as *Momento te esse mortalem* ("Remember that you are mortal"), you may be able to interpret it. If not, however, there are a great many dictionaries and reference books on the shelves of your local library.

In all likelihood, you will ocassionally find entire inscriptions in Latin. If this should occur, you should keep in mind that the way a word ends determines its meaning, and the ending of a single word can alter the meaning of an entire passage. Thus, you should never attempt to translate an entire Latin passage by yourself; instead, secure an expert to assist you.

Perhaps the greatest problem for the epitaph collector is the fact that there existed no standardized spelling in early America. If you could go back in time to the 1800's, you would discover that very few people could read, and fewer still were able to write. Thus, expecting our ancestors to possess accurate spelling abilities would have been totally out of the question, since the vast majority were barely able to spell their own names.

Indeed, most of the learned population who could in fact write did not take seriously the ideals of standard spelling. Instead, they spelled words precisely as they sounded - phonetically. This, coupled with the fact that stone cutters implemented their own regional accents into misspellings can make interpretation an extremely sticky problem for the tombstone genealogist.

A second consideration should be the fact that many of our ancestors came to settle in America from foreign lands, such as Germany, Africa, and Italy. Therefore, when records were etched into stone, scribes simply wrote what they heard from the deceased's relatives. Such must have been the case with the following inscription:

Lay me down beneaf de willers in de grass,
Where de branch'll go a-singin as it pass.
An w'en I's a-layin low
I kin heah it as I go
Sayin' Sleep, ma honey, tek yo res' at las'.

Obviously, in such a situation, you will be forced to call upon all of your knowledge and imagination in order to interpret passages simply because the words are misspelled.

When it comes to phonetically written words, a major problem can arise in the varied spelling of surnames on tombstones. In my own family tree, for example, I have found the name "Kremsreiter" spelled in no less than seventeen different ways, including Krimseiter, Kramshriter, Krumsriter, and even Cromswriter. In fact, to this day, I do not truly know the correct spelling, for I am forced to believe what my living relatives presently use. Therefore, don't be confused if you see the family name totally disassembled and reassembled upon the face of a grave marker. After all, the spelling of surnames was for decades at the mercy of those who chanced to etch it into stone.

This brings up the mistaken assumption of many epitaph researchers - that, if a name is not spelled precisely the way that it should be, then the person buried there cannot be your ancestor. Researchers who find, for example, a double "f" in the place of a "ph", or "ue" instead of "oo", should take notice, especially if both closely related spellings are found in the same cemetery or locale. The relationship is not always guaranteed; yet, neither is it certain when the spelling is exactly the same. Further investigation, however, is certainly warranted.

To the genealogical researcher, the rule for connecting a gap in a family tree with two variations of the same name is known as the law of *Idem Sonans*. In essence, it refers to the fact that it is not absolutely essential for a name to be spelled accurately in order to establish legal proof of relationship. Instead, if the name, as spelled, sounds nearly identical to the ear when pronounced in the accepted fashion, then it is accepted as being legal.

While conducting research into my own family history, I discovered that the Sinclair name had, over the centuries, been spelled as Sinclare, Sinkler, Sinklaire, and even St. Clair. These spelling variations seemed to have occurred when the family relocated from one region to another, though I have yet to determine whether or not it was intentionally carried out. Intent, however, has little to do with the end result of connecting the blood line, for the records speak for themselves. In a book entitled *The Zabriskie Family*, which is a historical outline written by George Olin Zabriskie, there were reportedly 123 spelling variations of the family name. If you should find only three or four, count yourself lucky. Whenever a genealogist or historian deals with writings or language from past generations, there most assuredly will be difficulties with semantics. The story of linguistic evolution is a tale filled with continual change. Hence, meanings and word usage have never been a static feature of life. They have undergone alterations in the past, they are undergoing alterations in the present, and they will undergo alterations in the future.

Early American graveyards seem to be literally filled with examples of varied language usage, as was the case with a number of New England epitaphs that speak of the deceased being "casually" killed or "casually" shot. This was not, in fact, as today's reader might think, a deliberately callous reference. Up-to-date dictionaries define "casual" to mean "unconcerned," "offhand," or "careless"; yet its meaning in early America was "unexpected," "unintentional," or "accidental." This is the type of problem epitaph researchers often encounter, and it certainly can cause us casual (in the early American definition of the word) difficulties.

Another oddly-worded inscription can be found on the grave marker of Lieutenant Mehuman Hindsdale, who died in Deerfield, Massachusetts, in 1736:

.....first male child born in this place
and was twice captivated by the Indian
Salvages.....

Terminology used during the 17th, 18th, and 19th centuries are no longer common today, and may seem strange to 20th century historians. However, in reality, such flawed memorials made perfect sense to those who wrote, etched, and read such inscriptions. In order to fully understand such passages, we must sometimes analyze their hidden meaning. With a little bit of historical research, using Funk & Wagnall's *New Standard Dictionary of the English Language*, we find our answer. The term "captivated," though now somewhat obsolete, means "to capture or subdue." Furthermore, the *Oxford English Dictionary* explains that the word "salvage" was once commonly used in place of "savage." Thus instead of humor we end up with a perfectly understandable explanation for the rather odd inscription.

"My glass is run" was a rather common expression during the period when hourglasses were used to calculate the inevitable passage of time. Hence, symbolically speaking, a person's life ended when the sands of time had run their course. The error of one stonecutter, however, offered an odd variation to the frequently written epitaph on the marker of James Ewins, who was buried in Forest Hill Cemetery, East Derry, New Hampshire, in 1781:

My glass is Rum.

The identical misspelled message appears over the grave of Ebenezer Tinney, who was laid to rest in a Grafton, Vermont cemetery in 1813. Still another reads:

Lord, she is thin.

Once again, we can only speculate on its meaning. It may have resulted from poor spelling or lack of space. Then again, perhaps the cutter was simply stating the truth.

In copying inscriptions from gravestones, therefore, it is always important to copy *verbatim ac litteratim*, word for word and letter for letter. This will eliminate any chance for error on your part. If, for example, the stone reads: "consort of," copy it that way, and do not substitute "wife" for "consort." The term "consort" signifies that the man or (in rare cases) the woman was living at the time of death, whereas "wife" does not necessarily mean the same. The term "relict," on the other hand, always refers to a widow (although occasionally, widower). Hence, you can determine that a wife had survived her husband. To the ordinary collector, this may seem insignificant; however, to a genealogist researching his or her family history, such a fact may prove invaluable.

This brings us to the point of semantics problems with terms referring to relationships among family members. The descriptive words "Junior" and "Senior," for example, usually make us think of the relationship between father and son. However, this is not always what was intended. On tombstones, these terms were merely used to distinguish between two persons with the same name, usually from two different generations, who resided in the same general region. More often than not, they spoke of an uncle and his nephew, rather than father and son. This can be particularly distressing to a researcher who finds three or more distinct generations with the same name. In time, when the eldest one died, a "Junior" was destined to become a "Senior," and thus created a good bit of "casual" discomfort for future genealogists.

As researchers, we must also be aware of the confusion between "in-law" relationships with "step" relationships. In past generations, stone cutters often claimed that an in-law connection existed when, in reality, it was nothing more than a step connection within a family. Any relationship created by legal means was usually identified as an in-law connection. Thus, a step-son was known as an in-law, and I do not even have to explain what difficulty this can cause for you in your search for long lost relatives. On tombstones, especially those from the 1600's, 1700's and early 1800's, other relationship terms were applied loosely as well. The words "brother", "sister", and "cousin" are some prime examples, though they are certainly not as significant as others.

In the Puritan settlements of Boston, Newton, and Salem, for example, "Brother Thomson" and "Sister Thomson" would, in all likelihood, not have referred to actual siblings, but rather a "Brother" and "Sister" of the church. Later, these same terms were often used to denote a marriage relationship. Hence, when a stone cutter wrote "Brother Thomson" and "Sister Thomson," he may have been referring to an actual brother and his wife, or vice versa. In fact, neither may have been related to the family at all, except by marriage. Hence, in understanding the above examples, it becomes rather puzzling for the genealogist to determine the truth of relationship.

The title of "cousin", on the other hand, is even more vague to an epitaph collector, for it was applied quite readily to almost any relationship outside of the immediate family. It may have been used when speaking of a nephew, niece, or marital spouse of any family member. Furthermore, it does not necessarily prove actual blood relationship at all, for it was sometimes applied to those connected only by marriage.

Whenever an epitaph refers to a "nephew" or "niece," it can cause real headaches for an ordinary researcher. As is the case with other relationship terms, they did not always carry the same connotations that we use today. "Nephew," for example, comes from the Latin "Nepos," which means, quite literally, "grandson." At the same time, "niece" is derived from the Latin "Neptis" which (you quessed it) is translated to mean "granddaughter." Thus, on a few rare headstones, "nephew" and "niece" may have totally different meanings than you might suspect. One fact on the plus side, however, is that by 1690, evolutionary changes had caused their earlier meanings to be almost entirely eliminated. Still, if you happen to find the actual Latin terms (Nepos or Neotis), you can rest assured that the phrasing can be literally translated to "grandson" or "granddaughter."

On rare occasions, you may run across the term "german" or "germane" inscribed on a headstone. Used when speaking of a family relationship, it is quite easy to decipher. "Sisters german," for example, would refer to children of the same parents, thus eliminating any possibility of them sharing a half-sister or step-sister relationship. Hence, it also follows the "cousins german" would indicate the actual children of brothers and sisters.

As you travel back in time through cemeteries scattered throughout America, you will undoubtedly come across epitaphs which use a variety of titles attached to a name. Keep in mind that from colonial times to the mid-1800's, many of these titles were simply the traditional use of British terms. Therefore, titles on tombstones were used to specify people of social rank, though the terms often lacked the precise connotations that had been attached to them in the mother country.

In England during the 1600's, for instance, any person who had "Esquire" (Esqr) attached to the end of his name was someone who held the distinct ability to bear arms. Esquires were, in the strict social sense, next in line after a knight, and deserved a specific amount of respect. As this title was imported to America, however, the meaning was altered slightly. Instead of denoting an arms bearer, it was simply attached to the most respected members of a particular community. Thus, on headstones, it may refer to a politician, physician, lawyer, judge, wealthy landowner, clergyman, or justice of the peace. Hence, the term does not actually pinpoint a specific fact about a person, though it may help to reinforce knowledge gained from other sources or documents.

Similarly, the American use of the title "Gentleman" (Gentln) does not possess the meaning that you might think. Instead it simply was used to signify a man of elite birth, who was socially situated one step down from an Esquire. Once again, the stone cutter may have only been referring to someone with a bit of high stature within local circles.

The term "Mrs." is normally used today when speaking of a married woman, but this was not always true in early America. More often than not it was applied to someone that was a member of the upper class, and had nothing to do with marital status. Thus, "Mrs. Anna Barnhard" may, in fact, be a title of courtesy that refers to a woman of "gentle" birth, married or single.

If you happen to read a stone that refers to a "goodman" or a "goodwife" (sometimes shortened to goody), you are once again climbing the social background ladder of knowledge. In each case, the title simply referred to a head of the household, either male or female respectively. Another title, most often used in the Southern portion of the United States, was "colonel." This in reality usually had nothing to do with military rank, but was simply applied to numerous old-time plantation owners.

Serious epitaph collectors should be aware that, from time to time, stone cutters implemented a variety of symbols in their work. Once again, this was usually done in order to abbreviate or save space. Some of the major symbols that you may encounter include:

> * - born
> (*) - illegitimately born
> X - baptized or christened
> O - engaged
> OO (with the two circles touching) - married
> O/O - divorced or separated
> O-O - common-law marriage

Finally, in the event that you encounter partially illegible inscriptions, it is a good idea to attempt a translation by filling in the missing portion by using what you can read. Furthermore, when you do so, make sure to place brackets ([,]) around the imagined portion of the transcription. Thus, your copy may read:

> [Sac]red to the memory of
> [Mich]ael Stevens
> [Wh]o expired
> [Marc]h 10, 1841
> [in] the 13th year
> [of hi]s life.

Whether or not you encounter all of the problems outlined above will depend, in large part, in which direction your family tree runs. If on the other hand you are merely a collector of tombstone literature, you will most certainly see many of them during your search. Hopefully, with the help of this chapter, you will be better equipped to understand the true meaning behind the various inscriptions that you uncover.

Chapter 7

Understanding Tombstone Art

Here lies the body of Richard Thomas
An inglishman by birth,
A Whig of '76.
By occupation a cooper,
Now food for worms.

Like an old rumpuncheon, marked,
numbered and shooked, he will be
raised again and finished by his
creator.... America, my adopted
country, my best advice to you is
this, Take care of your liberties.

As you pass among the dead in graveyards and cemeteries throughout America, do not overlook the abundance of sculptured art cut elegantly into stone: delicate flowers that seem real enough to emit a fine, fresh scent; crossed swords, telling us that the deceased was a high-ranking military man; or feathery barnyard roosters crowing a symbolic repentance for past improprieties. These stark, often lichen-covered images have evolved with the times, and will continue to do so. New designs are placed next to those that have been eagerly accepted by past generations. For example, modern-day torches positioned in an upside-down fashion stand near bows and arrows, each symbolizing mortality from a distinct era of American history.

Recently, during a search for my maternal grandmother's ancestors in a Saline, Michigan, cemetery, I discovered a gravestone carved with the picture of a well-known comic strip character. Covering the stone's entire face was an etching of Snoopy (of Peanuts fame), lying idly dormant as he is so often portrayed, atop his peaked doghouse. For today's historians, who are not unlike those who passed this way during the 17th and 18th centuries, such sculptures carry a message which often seems somewhat mysterious. It was quite apparent to me, however, that this unique display marked the grave of a youngster who found laughter and enjoyment in comic relief. Certainly, it was proof positive that times, even in death, are changing.

The earliest of America's symbolic carved headstone figures appeared in the New England area during the mid-1600's, at about the same time and place as epitaphs. Perhaps the oldest of all American etchings can be found in Old Wethersfield, Connecticut, on the headstone of Richard Chester, who died in 1648. Though crude and rigid, it depicts a dragon with a pointed nose and ears, its stick-like legs and tail bearing no resemblance to our modern-day conception of this legendary beast. Written historical records have told us that it was borrowed from the Chester family coat of arms.

Appreciating what they saw, other families mourning the dead soon followed suit, particularly in the Massachusetts Bay region. They carved their own unique coats of arms, escutcheons, and hatchments, each indicative of wealth and lineage. By the beginning of the 1690's, such proud family symbols had become commonplace, with their popularity spreading down along the Atlantic coastline and westward toward the fertile Ohio Valley. Such symbolic adaptations were to remain in use, especially in Rhode Island, for the next half century, when they were gradually replaced by more creative carvings.

In order to interpret the often hidden meanings behind stone carvings from the past, historians have found the need to conduct intensive research within books and periodicals. One such volume--dedicated to what author William West referred to as "symboleography"--has become almost obsolete, perhaps only available in the rarest of collections. With the passage of time, other references have also become extremely difficult to find. Hence, if you hope to investigate tombstone artwork thoroughly, you will need to rely heavily on your instincts, personal interpretations, and what you might learn in this chapter.

Early American gravestone artists were for the most part jacks-of-all-trades. Tombstone carving was not normally their full-time occupation. Therefore, they were forced to find more lucrative crafts, as farmers, blacksmiths, cobblers, braziers, surveyors, and even sailors. For still others, carving on headstones was simply an extension of an already established stone-related profession, such as bricklaying, masonry, or roofing. Hence, for most late 17th- and early 18th century tombstone artisans, carving portraits in stone was only a sideline or hobby. Simply put, they picked up their mallets and chisels only as the ocassion demanded.

In urban areas, a scattering of available written records tell us that a few of these untrained artists plied their hobby for a half-century or more. During that period, they often had a large and steady output, which eventually created an unforgettable reputation for past and present generations. Furthermore, pride dictated that they were seldom influenced by other carvers, and their finished products became somewhat distinctive. Consequently, competition among artists in well-populated areas offered the bereaved a wide choice of styles to choose from.

In the more rural regions, the sorrowing family was usually forced to accept the prowess of a local carver's style, whether they wanted to or not. Still, if the expense was not beyond the means, carvings could be purchased and transported from distant regions. Such merchandizing was normally handled by a "middleman" of sorts who, for a slight fee, would take care of all the arrangements.

The vast majority of these early stone sculptures possessed few qualities of true-to-life adaptation. The reason for this is quite easy to understand: hand engraving in stone was (and is) an extremely difficult task. Numerous would-be carvers were barely able to reproduce a single legible portrait. Others had the unique talent to carve an entire detailed scene in a primitive yet meaningful manner.

It is important to note that the artistic talent of an individual stonecutter was determined in large part by the quality of the stone he used. The smooth surface of close-grained slate, for example, permitted fine lines and delicate carvings. On the other hand, the coarser substance of both marble and sandstone were ideal for heavier designs.

Eventually, after a good deal of weeding, a small handful of master stone carvers began to emerge and flourish. Still, however, their images were not created from sheer imagination, as one might suspect, but came by way of copying other common funeral broadsides, primers, sermon books, and woodcuttings. Real creativity had not yet come to the forefront.

As a select few artists began to devote their entire lives to creating images on stone, however, they slowly began to develop an intricate visual language all their own. Trumpeting angels seemed to be floating weightlessly on heavenly clouds; intricate ships depicted lifetimes devoted to the sea; and skeletal death brought terror to the imaginations of the living. Yet despite the fact that personal style was beginning to take over, other creative endeavors continued to influence their work, including embroidery, weaving, wood-carving, blacksmithing, furniture building, and painting.

To keep up with the laws of supply and demand, a number of carvers developed their sculpturing craft into family-styled businesses. Fathers, wives, sons, and daughters worked together in a harmony of creativity, making stone markers which could be identified by specific cuts, figures, or trademarks. Eventually, the business would be passed on from one generation of a family to the next; this process of inheritance was repeated over and over again. Dynasties of tombstone artists were established, based mainly within the Massachusetts area; they included the Lamsons of Charleston, the Fosters of Dorchester, the Tingleys of Attleboro, and the Fishers of Wrentham.

Tradition became the main ingredient in the art of stone-carving during much of the 18th and early 19th centuries. Most carvers practiced their trade near the place of their birth, making a limited number of moves during their lengthy careers. Few were destined to be rewarded or remembered for their proficiency and creativity, and even fewer became wealthy from their work. Today the vast majority, which numbered one hundred or more over the course of two centuries, are buried in unkempt and unmarked graves. Many died destitute and forgotten, though they left behind a literal ocean of stone beauty.

Therefore, as you rub, trace, photograph, foil, and create moldings of your discoveries, keep in mind the mood and lifestyle of the carver. Most not only attempted to express their heartfelt emotions and artistic talents, but hoped to interpret the epitaphs which accompanied their finished work. Furthermore, all made an avid attempt to leave behind a moral lesson of learning to those who would later admire their carved teachings.

In essence, they were trying to tell us, without use of words, a small bit about their own lives, as well as that of the deceased. In studying the carvings, you will notice that the art-work can be divided into at least six distinct categories, including: (1) the fleeting passage of earthly time, (2) the inevitability of death as a warning to the living, (3) symbolic human and Christian characteristics, (4) the resurrection of the soul and the afterlife, (5) the proud station or occupation of the deceased, and (6) the often tragic cause of death.

In depicting the passage of time, which often seemed far too limited, the earliest symbol to appear on grave markers was the sand-filled hourglass. By the 1690's, everyone from young children to the very aged had been exposed to the "sands of time." Ministers, for example, used oversized versions while standing on their pulpits in order to limit their sermons to two or three hours; mothers used them in the kitchen while preparing the family meal; and schoolmasters incorporated them in timed mental exercises.

It should not seem odd, then, that such devices were inscribed upon the faces of tombstones. When the grains of sand had all gathered in the lower half, the life cycle had reached its completion. Fittingly, miniature hourglasses were etched upon the markers of young children, signifying their very brief lives. William Churcher, for example, saw fit to have just such a timepiece carved into the headstone of his five-year-old son, Richard, who died in 1683 and was buried in the Trinity Churchyard of New York City.

Shortly thereafter, stone carvers became a bit more inventive, attaching feathery wings to the hourglass shape. This, too, signified the fleeting passage of earthly time, and a splendid example can be found carved into the headstone of Thomas Kendel, who was buried in Wakefield, Massachusetts in 1681.

With the wide-spread acceptance of this symbolic tribute, wings were also attached to other carved figures: winged effigies depicted the human soul in flight; winged death's heads could be interpreted as the brief existence of mortality; flying birds showed the flight of the human soul from earth: and winged roses symbolized the brevity of earthly life.

As the modern world began to replace outdated devices in the real world, so, too, did modern symbolism representing the passage of time appear on gravestones. In Woodstock, Connecticut, for example, we find one of only two carved clocks known to exist. Sculpted in 1752, it replaced the hourglass, and its hands tell us that six o'clock was the symbolic hour of death.

In Puritan New England, newlyweds often customarily planted a pair of young "marriage trees." These trees would be positioned just outside of the entryway to a recently constructed home, one on either side, and symbolized the bonding of marriage. On rare occasions, when one of these marriage partners was "cut down" in the prime of life, his or her tombstone would depict a marriage tree recently felled by the powerful hand of God. Such a scene can be found on the headstone of Elizabeth Norton, in Durham, Connecticut, which was carved in 1751.

Time eventually took human form, as numerous New England stone carvers began to portray Father Time himself. Inevitably, he was an aging man sporting a lengthy beard, dressed in a flowing robe, clenching a sharpened scythe, and carefully cradling an hourglass in his arms. On a number of early headstones, in fact, the sand-filled hourglass would be delicately balanced at the peak of Father Time's head, as a sign of the precarious and fragile nature of life itself. Such an arrangement is well-preserved on the tombstone of Timothy Lindall, who died in 1698/9, and was buried in Salem, Massachusetts.

For the most part, stone artists employed everyday items within their carvings to get their point across. An ordinary candle, for example, standing upright on a small nightstand, was sometimes sculpted. Such an arrangement was typically found in a person's sleeping guarters during the 17th and 18th centuries, with the table positioned in such a way that the candle was within arm's reach. Whenever the occupant decided that it was time to retire for the night, he would simply douse the flame with a small snuffer.

Hence, it seemed quite natural for a candle and snuffer to appear on a person's headstone, which would symbolize the end of a life. More often than not, a combination of symbols depicting the passage of time would appear upon a tombstone. On a slate dedicated to Joseph Tapping, for instance, which was placed near the entrance of King's Chapel Burial Ground in Boston in 1678, Father Time is desperately attempting to stop skeletal Death from snuffing out the candle of life.

Mortality was depicted in a variety of ways on grave markers, each preaching the plain truth that death is unavoidable. Closed coffins, Death's darts, imps, skeletons, and even pallbearers were etched into stone, each signifying the inevitability of life's cessation. Perhaps the most widely used of these symbols was the death's head, which was carved in numerous fashions, depending on the artist's personal conception of dying. To many, he was a rather happy being; to others, he seemed sad and forlorn. On rare ocassions, he was even depicted as a blankly staring skull, situated above crossed bones. Whatever his facial expression might be, however, he was always disdained, and most often appeared with open wings.

As symbolism of death evolved, the skull was replaced by the entire skeleton. Often, such figures carried "darts of death," arrows, and even javelins, which were aimed at the unsuspecting human form of the living. Evidently, Thomas Roberts was surprised by Death, for his tombstone, which stands in a Newburyport, Massachusetts graveyard shows him being stabbed in the back by a skeleton holding a sharpened spear.

Aside from skeletal Death himself, other symbols soon became prevalent in representing mortality, the vast majority of which were related to the actual burial process. Perhaps the most popular carving of all was the wooden coffin, closed and ready for interment. Occasionally, an open coffin was sculpted by the stonecutter, perhaps to depict what death might look like to the living. For example, the coffin carved into Mary Harvey's stone in Deerfield, Massachusetts, remains forever thrust open, and shows that she was buried with an infant daughter in her arms in 1785.

The shovel, pickaxe, spade, and pall were also used as a constant reminder to the living that "as I am now, so you shall be."

In fact, the survivors of Captain Jonathan Poole of Wakefield, Massachusetts displayed all of these implements on his tombstone when he was buried in 1678. There are numerous similar examples found throughout the colonial New England region.

According to scripture, the Apostle Peter was forced to realize his sin of denying Christ when he heard the distant crowing of a cock. One stone cutter from Longmeadow, Massachusetts, incorporated these barnyard critters on grave markers in an attempt to warn us of impending doom. His symbolic message tells us that we would be well-advised to repent our mortal wrongs before it is too late. A well-preserved example of the crowing rooster can still be seen on the brownstone marker of Naomi Woolworth, who was buried in a local Longmeadow streetside cemetery in 1760.

Human emotions and Christian characteristics often took precedence over more subtle earthly symbols on early-day grave markers. Angels, for example, were portrayed as escorts to lead the deceased toward the rewards of heaven; open bibles depicted resurrection through the holy words of the scriptures; a tall stack of books represented knowledge and insight; and female breasts signified the divine nourishment of the eternal soul.

Perhaps the most widely used portrait related to goodness and the Christian way of life was that of the vine creeping ever upward toward the heavens; when bunches of grapes were attached to the vines, it represented wine and the symbolic blood of Christ. An intricately crafted example of this is found on the stone of Lieutenant William Hercy, erected in Wakefield in 1689.

From time to time, birds were placed in the grape vines, standing elegantly near the ripened fruit. Historians, including Harriette Merrifield Forbes, explained that these winged creatures "signified the soul partaking in celestial food." If the bird in question happened to be an eagle, it represented the "heavenly conveyor." Peacocks, on the other hand, symbolized immortality and goodness, while doves conveyed the quality of Christian purity and devotion. In Providence, Rhode Island, we find the Harris family crest motif--three doves placed amid a sprawling vine--on the 1729 grave marker of Job Harris. Evidently, the family believed that he was destined for blessed immortality in the afterlife.

Keep in mind that grapevines were not the only type of plant life sculpted to represent Christian qualities. The weeping willow tree was widely used during the 19th century to signify earthly sadness; the thistle, of Scottish origin, indicated that the deceased would forever be remembered; palms suggested victory over death by those destined for a better afterlife; and gourds symbolized the passing away of all earthly worries and cares.

For the most part, fully branching trees were carved to represent the continuing tree of life, or the passing on of human characteristics from one generation to the next. In a small, wooded graveyard in Grafton, Vermont, you can find the curious joint burial spot memorializing Rebecca Park and her fourteen children. In this case, the stone cutter employed a fitting marker fashioned from cloudy gray slate. Using a compass, he artistically drew thirteen tiny faces blossoming from the extended branches of the eternal tree. Interestingly enough, the face of the fourteenth child was separated from the others, detached from the tree, and placed at the center of the stone. Why, we do not know, but perhaps it was because one of the Park children was buried elsewhere. Whatever the reason, the unusual arrangement makes this one of the most unique stones in existence.

Animals were also incorporated by early stone artists to convey Christian characteristics of the recently deceased. Lambs symbolized innocence, while lions were indicative of braveness and strength. Other of God's creatures carved into stone included deer, dogs, and even squirrels, though their true symbolic meaning has since been forgotten. Perhaps they were meant to signify hobbies, interests, or were simply part of a family's crest.

Also important to the living were symbolic figures of the afterlife, or the eventual destination of the soul. The promised land, as we know it, was one "of wheat and barley and vines and fig trees and pomegranates." Therefore, it seems logical that each of these should be used by New England stone carvers to represent prosperity and happiness in the next world.

Obviously, resurrection of the human essence into heaven was first and foremost in the minds of the living. Therefore, a wide variety of symbols was incorporated to represent this message, including buds, butterflies, hooped snakes, and the hand of God pointing upward. Yet, perhaps the most readily recognized of all resurrection figures was, and still is, represented by border motifs of an abundant crop. Sheaves of wheat, for example, pointed toward the divine harvest of the human soul; garlands of flowers signified a triumph over death; and baskets of ripened fruit proved that the deceased would find an eternal plenty in heaven. Such carvings persisted well into the 1800's, and are sometimes still used today.

Common on the face of headstones even today is the portrait of a lone trumpet, which one writer points out brings to mind the words of the scripture: "The trumpet shall sound and the dead be raised incorruptible." A great number of these appear throughout the Massachusetts area, and are likely the work of a single artist or a family of stone carvers. In Petersborough, New Hampshire, in fact, the major tourist attraction within the confines of the East Hill Cemetery is the intricate carving of the angel Gabriel blowing his fetching bugle over the grave of Charles Stuart.

Later, we see the development of more worldly symbols on headstones, such as the rising sun, the earth, the moon, and the stars. On one such stone, dedicated to an infant in Berlin Center, New York, we find a tiny hand pointing upward toward a single star, inscribed with the words "Gone Home." On another, which commemorates Jacob Repass in St. John's Churchyard, Wytheville, Virginia, the rays of the sun reach toward heavenly resurrection. And in Bowmansville, Pennsylvania, there appears a smiling half-moon flanked by a pair of oversized stars.

It is evident, due to both their verses and their artwork, that stone carvers were not always quite certain what death held in store for the recently departed. For example, bats in flight have been interpreted by experts to represent the damnation of hell; imps suggested that the next life was somewhat uncertain; and no explanation whatsoever is necessary for a hand pointing downward. Evidently, eternal bliss was not always in the cards of the future.

Furthermore, let us not forget that a few of the deceased believed in no resurrection of the soul at all. Rumor has it that Cy Deeter, of Woodington, Ohio, opted to become an atheist because of the excessive physical attraction of a local minister to his wife. When Hattie, his wife, died in 1876, he placed the following caustic message over her grave:

> There is no God. Man has no soul.
> Life ends forever at death. The human
> race has advanced, not on account of
> the Church, but in spite of it.
> Civilization is due to science and
> not to Christianity. Does a Catholic priest
> or a preacher realize how unnecessary they
> are on earth? I hope there is a hell for
> all those hell fire preachers.

Even before Deeter's own death, vengeful citizens living near the Darke County community became insensed with his accusations. After his death, they gradually began to chip small pieces of the tombstone away. Today, nothing of the monument's sculpted artwork still exists.

As was the case with a great number of epitaphs, carvings often described the station or occupation of the deceased. Quite likely, the first of these to appear was the family coat-of-arms, etched proudly into the center of a stone's face for all the world to see. The stone dedicated to Captain John Fowle is considered by many to be one of the most artistic creations in all of New England. Standing regally in the Phipps Street Burial Ground in Charlestown, Massachusetts, it depicts a ferocious lion with clawed paws extended in an attack stance, and tail curled upward in retaliation.

Military men, adorned handsomely in full uniform, were sculpted on flat tombstones and tablestones with the same proficient care. A fine example is that of Captain Anthony Gwyn, who was buried in St. Paul's Churchyard, Newburyport, Massachusetts. With his button-down coat, three-cornered army hat, and sharpened sword, he seems a fine specimen for any regiment - in spite of the fact that he was 80 years old when he died on December 29, 1776.

Other military paraphernalia etched forever into grave markers includes bugles, crossed swords, eagles, muskets, and a variety of field artillery. In New York City's Trinity Churchyard, for example, we find three cannons at the top of Daniel Rowls Carpenter's gravestone. Its weathered and eroded inscription records that "He was a member of the Company of Officers sent to this place by the Honorable Boared [sic] of Ordinance under the direction of Major Dixon: Chief engineer of America."

Occasionally, we find a marker whose etching depicts a particular incident during military conflict. During the Civil War, James J. Andrews and twenty-one other Union soldiers attempted to sneak across enemy lines into Georgia. Their mission was to capture a Confederate train at Big Shanty. However, as fate would have it, unusually wet weather hindered their journey. Andrews and seven others were captured and hanged for their daring exploit. Today, a miniature bronze reproduction of the commandeered Western and Atlantic engine surmounts a marble pedestal in the National Cemetery, Chattanooga, Tennessee. Below is inscribed the names of the eight who were executed, of eight others who made a successful escape, and of six who were later freed in a prisoner-of-war exchange.

Just as military trappings symbolized the proud heritage of America's soldiers, the tall-masted wooden ship memorialized the navy, and seamen in general. Perhaps the most intricate example of all can be seen in a small graveyard in Deep River, Connecticut. The front carving on an oversized marble obelisk, which was carved in 1851, shows a three-masted vessel, with not less than fifteen separate sails, taut ropes, and the ship's flag.

Lieutenant Jabez Smith died on June 28, 1780, and was laid to rest in the Granary at Boston. Just a few days earlier, this brave seafarer had been critically wounded while doing battle with a British vessel off the coast of Bermuda. Even today, the stars and stripes fly above the stern of his ship, the *Trumbull*, which is etched into his marker. Above the ship are the following words:

Anchored in the Haven of Rest.

It was not only soldiers and seafarers who were forever memorialized in stone adorned in the full dress of their profession. Ministers can often be recognized by their tight collars, flowing robes, or even armbands, as is the case with the Reverend Grindall Rawson, who was buried in Mendon, Massachusetts, in 1715.

Perhaps the most intricately-etched stone of all is one dedicated to the Reverend John Angier, which stands in the Old Grave Yard of East Bridgewater, Massachusetts. Sculpted in 1787, the slate tympanum depicts Angier in full dress standing behind his five-sided wooden pulpit preaching his final sermon. Nestled in front of him is a ceremonial "sermon pillow," upon which lies an open prayer book held firmly in the reverend's right hand.

Others have left their occupational mark on their tombstones as well. While walking among the stones in Bristol, Rhode Island's Juniper Hill Cemetery a few summers ago, I happened upon a fine slate memorial dedicated to Dr. Thomas Munro. I found an etching of the young doctor from a side profile, with his hands extended in an appropriate healing gesture.

Portraits of tragic death have long been a part of the stone cutter's artistic prowess throughout America, and numerous markers depict victims of chance and circumstance. One such episode is recorded on a stone commemorating Mary Points in a rural cemetery near Aberdeen, Mississippi. In January of 1852, she was burned to death when her flowing skirts accidentally caught fire. Her marker shows an attractive woman's face engulfed by sweeping flames.

In Pepperell Center, Massachusetts, stands a small stone which depicts the startled face of a youngster named Aaron Bowers, who remains permanently transfixed with his tiny arms raised upward in a futile effort to ward off a load of falling lumber. Below, the words complete the story by explaining that young Aaron was "Instantly killed by a Stock of boards."

A similar tragedy occurred in Hanover Center, Massachusetts, in 1768, which was vividly portrayed on a gravestone dedicated to John Stockbridge. It is more than clear that he was laid low by a tree which he was chopping down, for the sculpture depicts a fallen trunk with Stockbridge caught beneath its weight. Significantly, the sun is shown shining brilliantly overhead, a

91

saddened face etched into its circular form. Directly below, the fateful axe lies beside the trapped victim. His epitaph records that he was:

> ...of fair and unblemished character, in deportment and verulous....whose mortality has rendered the male issue of that branch of that respectable family extinct.... His death was sudden, premature, awfull and violent. Providentially occasioned by the fall of a tree....No sums can purchase such a grant that man shall never die.

Very little significance was given to such gravestones during the American colonial period. Hence, it is not surprising that they are rarely mentioned by contemporary writers. Yet, such sculptures recorded history in a truly amazing fashion, and should be remembered for generations to come. Below is a list of headstone motifs that figure prominently in graveyards throughout the country:

> Anchors - Sailing, seafaring, navy (18th-19th centuries)
> Angels - Heavenly guides (18th-19th centuries)
> Arches - Victory in death (18th-19th centuries)
> Arrows - Mortality (17th-18th centuries)
> Bats - Hell (18th century)
> Bibles - Resurrection, scriptures, the religious profession (18th-19th centuries)
> Birds in flight - Passage of the soul into Heaven (18th-19th centuries)
> Books - Intelligence, knowledge, wisdom (19th century)
> Bouquets - Grief, sorrow (19th century)
> Branches - Life cycle (18th-19th centuries)
> Branches, severed - Mortality (18th century)
> Breasts - The nourishment of the soul (17th century)
> Bugles - Military profession, resurrection (18th-19th centuries)
> Butterflies - Afterlife, rebirth (19th century)
> Candles, snuffed - Mortality, time (17th century)
> Clocks - Passage of time, mortality, time of death (18th century)
> Clouds - Heavenly rewards (18th century)
> Coats of arms - Lineage, status, nobility (17th-18th centuries)
> Coffins - Mortality (17th-18th centuries)
> Coffins, empty - Unoccupied grave (17th-18th centuries)

Crests - Lineage, status, nobility (17th-18th centuries)
Crowns - Christian fortitude, righteousness (18th century)
Darts - Mortality (17th-18th centuries)
Doves - Purity of the soul (18th-19th centuries)
Death's heads, winged - Mortality (17th-18th centuries)
Eagles - Heavenly guide, nationalism, military profession,
    Civil War casualty (18th-19th centuries)
Effigies - Human soul (18th century)
Effigies, crowned - Righteousness, goodness (18th cen-
    tury)
Effigies, winged - Flight of the soul (18th century)
Eyes - God's watchful eye (19th century)
Father Time - Passage of time (17th-18th centuries)
Field artillery - Military profession (18th-19th centuries)
Flower buds - Birth, beginning of a new life (18th cen-
    tury)
Flowers - Brevity of human existence, sorrow, grief
    (18th-19th centuries)
Fruit - Everlasting plenty (17th-18th centuries)
Garlands - Victory in death (18th-19th centuries)
God - Judgement (18th century)
Gourds - Passing of all earthly cares (17th-18th centuries)
Imps - Mortality, an uncertain afterlife (17th century)
Hand of God, chopping - Mortality, sudden death (18th
    century)
Hands, outstretched - Healing power, physician (18th-19th
    centuries)
Hand, pointing downward - The way to Hell (19th cen-
    tury)
Hand, pointing upward - Rewards of Heaven (19th cen-
    tury)
Hands, folded - Prayer, scripture, devotion (18th-19th
    centuries)
Handshake - Farewell to earthly matters (19th century)
Hearts - Blissful soul, love of God (18th-19th centuries)
Horns - Resurrection (18th century)
Hourglasses - Passage of time (17th-18th centuries)
Hourglasses, winged - Swift passage of time (17th-18th
    centuries)
Lambs - Innocence (19th century)
Lamps - Eternal Heavenly light (19th century)
Moon - Reward of resurrection (18th-19th centuries)
Muskets - Military profession, hunting profession (18th-
    19th centuries)
Noah's Ark - Protection, salvation (18th-19th centuries)

Orbs as effigies - Human soul (18th-19th centuries)
Pallbearers - Mortality (17th-18th centuries)
Palls - Mortality (17th-18th centuries)
Palms - Victory in death (18th-19th centuries)
Peacocks - Immortality, goodness (18th century)
Picks - Mortality (17th century)
Portals - Passage into Heaven (17th-18th centuries)
Portraits - Likeness of the deceased (18th-19th centuries)
Pulpit - Religious profession (17th-18th centuries)
Roosters - Repentance (18th century)
Roses - Sorrow, grief, brevity of life (18th-19th centuries)
Scythes - Time, the divine harvest (17th-18th centuries)
Shells - Life, birth (18th-19th centuries)
Ships - Seafaring profession (18th-19th centuries)
Shovels - Mortality (17th century)
Shrines - Wisdom, knowledge (18th-19th centuries)
Skeletons - Mortality (17th-18th centuries)
Skulls - Mortality (17th-18th centuries)
Snake, hooped - Eternity (18th-19th centuries)
Snakes - Temptation (18th-19th centuries)
Stars - Reward of resurrection (18th-19th centuries)
Stations in life - Occupation of the deceased (18th-19th
         centuries)
Sun - Reward of resurrection (18th-19th century)
Swords - Military profession (17th-18th centuries)
Swords, crossed - Ranking military person (18th century)
Thistles - Mortality (18th century)
Tombs - Mortality (18th-19th centuries)
Torches, upside-down - Mortality (19th century)
Train - Engineer's profession (19th century)
Trees - Life cycle, tree of life (18th century)
Trumpeters - Heralds of resurrection (18th century)
Urns - Mortality, an occupied grave (19th century)
Vines - Wine, blood of Christ (18th century)
Wheat - Time, the divine harvest (19th century)
Willows - Sorrow, grief, sadness (19th century)
Wreaths - Victory in death (18th-19th centuries)

Chapter 8

Tombstone Highlighting, Chalking, & Tracing

> I have chosen to have my ashes placed here
> because I revere this ancient cemetery and the
> historic church across the way by which it is
> governed. And I have selected the rough boulder
> which marks this spot because it was found
> imbedded in the trail leading through the woods
> on my own Sunshine Hill, where I have passed so
> many happy years, and because my dog Teddy
> and I have walked it so often.

If you are compelled to read, interpret, and contemplate each individual epitaph as you walk along a cemetery row, you will discover that worn and weathered inscriptions are quite common. Often, they are extremely difficult to transcribe at first glance, and may take some decided effort on your part to figure out. Normally, this is due to any one of a number of common problems, including water streaks and stains, lichen growing in the cracks and crevices of the stone, salt deposits, damage from people, and natural wearing of the epitaph's incisions. Yet, despite the difficulties you may have in deciphering a headstone's words, there are a number of steps that you might take in order to record them.

While making my way a through North Cemetery in Vernon, Vermont a few years ago, I happened upon a hard-to-read epitaph. Studying it closely by rubbing my fingers across the surface, I could just barely make out the name of Jonathan Tute, who had died at the tender age of 14 in 1763. Immediately, my inquisitive mind went into action, and I pondered what might have caused the unfortunate death of young Jonathan. Did he die from some accidental happening, perhaps, or was he a victim of small-pox? Maybe he was the victim of some hideous crime?

Using a technique known as rubbing, which I had learned from my many hours of experimenting with tombstones and which is detailed in chapter 10, I began to make progress with the legibility of the first few words of the damaged inscription. Soon, four lines of young Tute's epitaph were a bit more legible:

> But tho' His Spirits fled on high
> His body mould'ring here must lie
> Behold the amazing alteration
> Effected by Inoculation....

Still, the rest of the message was giving me some difficulty. Discouraged by the fact that two more lines seemed almost impossible to transcribe, I cleaned the lichen-infested stone with a damp rag and a soft-bristled toothbrush. Eventually, I was able to make out the final two lines, which blatantly proclaimed:

> The means Employed his Life to save
> Hurried Him Headlong to the Grave.

Finally, the epitaph made sense. Obviously, it was a local doctor's devastating inoculation procedure that had caused the 14-year-old's untimely death.

Jonathan Tute's memorial had been worn nearly smooth by the elements, and the incisions that remained were filled with dirt and lichen. Such problems, however, can be overcome by a few special techniques outlined in the chapters that follow.

Even when a stone's words are cut deep enough to withstand the elements, other impeding factors may enter into the picture. Most often, the readability of a particular inscription depends heavily on the time of day, weather conditions, or the season. Direct sun, for example, can cause the epitaph's cuts to be flooded with too much light. Cloudy, overcast skies, on the other hand, provide an inadequate amount of natural light for sound tombstone readings. Under such conditions, a researcher must sometimes decide to wait for the sun's rays to appear, which will provide more adequate shadows within a stone's incisions.

Studying the effects of sunlight on a variety of headstones will emphasize the importance of the angle of illumination. Ideally, the beams of collimated light, such as those cast by an early morning or late afternoon sun, will cast sharp-edged shadows. Subsequently, you will be able to see acute forms, planes, textures, and incisions. Indeed, a sharply angling sun will make shadows form within the shallow lines of the epitaph, making it far more easy to read.

Such was the case during my annual autumn journey through New Hampshire several years ago. As always, I stopped often to picnic in a variety of burial sites, taking in the epitaphs as well as the multi-colored scenery surrounding the cemeteries. On one particularly cloudy Thursday, in the Old Washington Street Cemetery located in Keene, I happened upon a stone dedicated to Mrs. Elizabeth Blake. Though I could clearly see the majority of the epitaph, a brief message at ground level had me somewhat perplexed. Three short lines seemed nearly impossible to read, due to the heavy, diffused shadows of the overcast skies.

The following weekend was far more clear, so I took the time to return to the cemetery. Late in the afternoon, as the sun's rays bore down on that same stone, I found that the incisions were much more decisive. There, having nothing to do with the epitaph itself, was a brief message from the man who had cut the stone:

Made by Mose
Wright of Rockingham
Vt. Price 8 dollars.

Since that time, I have learned to use sunlight and shadow to my advantage on a number of tombstone expeditions.

Daytime weather conditions, however, are certainly not the only factors that might impede your progress as an epitaph researcher. If, for example, after examining a headstone closely under the angling rays of afternoon sunlight, you discover that no shadows are cast within a particular stone's incisions, do not give up hope. It may simply be neccesary to either highlight the entire face of the stone or to carefully trace the letters one by one.

While pursuing the hobby of epitaph highlighting or tracing, you would be well-advised not to wear your Sunday best, since you will literally be "groveling" in the dirt, weeds, and grass. Furthermore, you should come to the cemetery equipped to handle any and all situations. Since tombstones have been known to settle, weather, fall, attract dirt and lichen, or become overgrown in thick grasses and weeds, you should bring along a number of essential tools. These include grass trimmers, a small hand saw, a trowel or spade, a soft-bristled brush, a new toothbrush, a large container full of water, and plenty of clean rags.

First, use the grass trimmers to clear away any weeds and tall grasses that might have grown up around the stone. Don't hesitate to cut it right down to ground level. If any grass or weed strands are touching the stone itself, however, don't take the chance of scratching it with the metal trimmers; instead, pull them completely out by the roots. In any event, give yourself plenty of room to work around the marker's face.

If, as so often happens, bushes and small trees have crowded in around the grave marker, you may have to use your trimmers and hand-saw to remove some of their branches. It goes without saying that you should never remove plants that have been intentionally placed around a tombstone as memorial offerings. Flowers, small evergreens, and ferns should be left intact. Instead, simply trim away any protruding branches that may hinder your hobby, making sure that all cuts are uniform and even. After all, you wouldn't want to deface a plot that has been meticulously and lovingly landscaped by relatives or friends of the deceased.

There are a number of reasons, such as wind, flooding, tree roots, or even vandalism, that may cause a gravestone to shift its original position. Often, such distressed markers will be leaning precariously, will be broken into a number of smaller pieces, or may have already fallen over completely. Under no circumstances should you ever attempt to right a grave marker by assembling broken chunks or moving it back into place. Not only might you hurt yourself in the process, but a fragile, aging stone may break apart even more. Leave it where nature's forces or fate intended it to be, and choose another stone that is in better condition. If the damaged marker happens to be one that memorializes a long-lost relative, complete your investigation the best way possible without altering its position.

You may notice, however, that a specific tombstone is standing upright, but has settled passively into the soft earth. Quite possibly, you may further determine that a portion of the inscription is now below the surface of the ground. Such was the situation which I personally came across in my search for my paternal great-grandfather and great-grandmother.

Within the confines a a small church cemetery, located in Beal City, Michigan, and known as St. Joseph The Worker, are the many remains of my relatives. It was here, scattered among approximately 300 or more grave markers, that I traveled to find John Schafer and his wife, Katherine. A locally published centennial historical edition informed me that they had come from Westphalia, Michigan, in 1882. During the next ten years, John practiced the trade of mason, and he assisted in the construction of a great many of the farm community's oldest homes. Sadly, while he was riding aboard a wagon east of town he was killed by a toppling load of lumber.

After a brief bit of searching, I came upon John's weathered headstone. During the decades since his death, a rather intrusive elm tree had pushed the marker up on one corner, causing it to tilt precariously to one side. There was nothing I could do for the stone, however, due to its fragile condition.

Tree roots and trunks, however, are not the only cause of jostled grave markers. Similar circumstances seem to have occurred quite often on older, 17th- and 18th-century stone markers, due to the fact that cement base foundations had not yet come into use. If you discover that this is indeed the case, you may find (as I did) that an excavation job is in order.

Excavating a gravestone from the ravages of time is not an easy task, for you must be very careful not to make matters worse. First, use the trowel or spade to carefully dig the dirt out from around the base of the marker's face, making certain that you don't scrape or chip the stone in the process. Furthermore, take care to avoid digging more than a few inches down; nor should you, under any circumstances, dig beneath the stone, for hardened, packed dirt is needed to maintain its correct upright posture.

If you go down deep enough, you should be able to feel the concave edges of the epitaph's incisions with your fingertips. Keep digging until you can feel no more cuts in the stone, making sure to clear enough space to complete your highlighting or tracing. And after you are completely finished, make sure that you refill the hole, leaving the ground the way you found it. As an added measure, pack the dirt down firmly with your foot.

After you have carefully excavated enough dirt so that the inscription is completely exposed, you must take the time to clean the stone's face. First, moisten the soft-bristled brush by soaking it a few minutes in a bucket of water. Take the time to resoak it often as you work so that the bristles do not become too dry and abrasive. Move the brush in a back-and-forth motion across the face of the stone, applying only a moderate amount of pressure. This should result in the removal of all bits of lichen and dirt that may be clinging to the surface. Under absolutely no circumstances, however, should you ever clean the surface of a headstone with a wire brush; it will scratch and mar the face beyond recognition. One further note: be extra gentle with any rough-surfaced sandstone or slate markers that are cracked. Both of these varieties will tend to break away and chip quite easily, and you will become a vandal rather than a researcher.

Next, take your toothbrush and clean each intricate incision that continues to be clogged with debris. This may be a painstakingly slow and tedious procedure, but look at the bright side: you are carrying out a service that has not been done for decades. And furthermore, it is highly improbable that anyone will take the time and effort to complete such an extensive cleaning job again for many years to come. Besides, you can feel good about the fact that you are clearing the way for other future epitaph readers.

Finally, dampen a rag with water and wipe the face of the stone free of all remaining particles of dirt. I don't recommend using any sort of man-made cleaning agents or chemicals on the face of the stone. Not only are they abrasive and, therefore, potentially disfiguring, but they may leave a dark stain over the original coloration of the marker. After all, you didn't come here to alter the stone, only to create the illusion of legibility for posterity's sake. Now you are ready to try your hand at highlighting or tracing, whichever seems more appropriate for a particular occasion.

Simply put, tombstone highlighting is a temporary method of reinforcing the background surrounding a headstone's writings and sculptures. The easiest method of highlighting that I have found is to incorporate materials that are most readily available. In fact, all you really need is your own two hands and a small bucket of water.

Using your fingers or, for the more civilized, one of the small digging utensils you brought along, turn up the ground surrounding the marker. In fact, you may have already done so during your excavation maneuver. If so, simply employ the dirt that you have already turned. Carefully sift out all grass, pebbles, and stones that may be polluting your freshly-turned earth, thus creating a mound of "clean" dirt. In this way, you will avoid scratching or chipping the face of the stone. If it has been unusually dry in recent days, you may wish to sprinkle a few drops of water on your pile, turning it into a slightly moistened mud-mound. Next, smear the damp dirt over the face of the stone with your hand, making certain to rub latitudinally as you progress.

Use a slight bit of muscle as you work - about the same amount you might use if you were shaping a clay figure that was just beginning to harden. Almost instantly, you'll notice that the slightly moistened dirt will begin to adhere to the crevices of the headstone. Cover the incisions carefully, pushing mud into each individual cut. Make sure that the clinging action is uniform over the entire face. Keep in mind that additional water will cause the dirt to stick firmly, while too much may make it too heavy to withstand the force of gravity.

Finally, dip your hand in the bucket of water and splash a small amount over the marker's surface. Wash away the dirt particles that are stuck to the background of the face by rubbing your dampened hand over the surface. Take care that you don't make the stone too wet - otherwise, you will remove the mud imbedded in the stone's incisions, thus ruining your work.

Soon, if carried out in the correct manner, you will have created a simple mud mold. Notice how the lighter background now surrounding the darker mud-packed incisions causes the lettering to stand out much more clearly. And, clean-up of the stone is simple once you have completed your transcription: the drying dirt will easily wash away with a wet rag or be diluted during the next heavy downpour. Since most researchers want to leave the stones exactly as they find them, I would recommend the use of your toothbrush once again. It will make the next researcher's job that much easier in the future.

Mud highlighting works best with light-colored stones, such as tan, red, or bluish-gray sandstone, quartzite, or schist. The greater the contrast in color between the dirt and the marker, the greater degree the lettering will stand out against the darkened background. Furthermore, the sand grain particles of these stones allows the mud to cling more firmly to the incisions of the marker.

Though I do not often use the "mud mold" highlighting technique, I have found that it comes in quite handy on the spur of the moment. While making the connecting drive from Hartford to Norwich, Connecticut, last summer, I was drawn to a brief pause by old Wethersfield's picturesque scenery. Once I had stopped the car and had begun a brisk walk through town, I happened upon Village Cemetery. There, among a number of other slate and sandstone markers, I found an epitaph dedicated to a mother and her children.

Unable to read the entire inscription, I used a nearby hand-pump to secure water in a plastic tub, dampened the soft earth surrounding the grave, and commenced rubbing the dirt into the stone's crevices. Ever so slowly, a tale of domestic tragedy began to appear:

> Here lie Interred Mrs. Lydia Beadle
> Aged 32 years, Ansell Lothrop Elizabeth
> Lydia & Mary Beadle her children; the eldest
> aged 11 and the youngest 6 years, who,
> on the morning of the 11th day of Dec'r,
> 1782, Fell by the hands of William
> Beadle, an infatuated Man, who closed
> the horrid sacrafice of his Wife and Children
> with his own destruction.

For those of you who do not wish to "get down and dirty" with natural elements that are near at hand, a second highlighting method is available. Known as chalking, it will save you the trouble of washing caked dirt from your digits, will keep you safe from getting mud under your fingernails, and may provide a much better method of deciphering worn and weathered epitaphs. Besides, it is the preferred method whenever you encounter darker stones, such as slate and brownstone.

Before going out on your first chalking expedition, visit your local art retailer, office supply house, or educational equipment outlet. Purchase a large supply of ordinary white or multicolored chalk, which is both inexpensive and easy to find. I would recommend the type that is fat-bodied, so that the job will not cause injury (as you will soon understand).

Now, when you have located the tombstone of your choice, take the necessary excavation steps described earlier in this chapter. Using the long, side edge of the chalk, rub firmly over the entire face of the stone. Use more than one piece if necessary, for the chalk will soon become flattened and will eventually become exhausted. If you aren't careful you will find that your knuckles will become scraped and raw by accidentally rubbing against the coarse surface of the stone. Sandpapered skin is no laughing matter!

The first time that I incorporated the chalking method to highlight a gravestone was during a vacation in New Jersey. There, in a quaint little burial site known as the Baptist Churchyard, located in the small village of Hamilton Square, I came upon a marker dedicated to a four year old member of the Cubberly family who had died in 1843. The epitaph told of a tragic and fatal accident:

> The boiling coffee did on me fall,
> And by it I was slain,
> But Christ has brought me liberty,
> And in Him I'll rise again.

The result of chalking the face of the youngster's tombstone left me with exactly the opposite effect of the mud-packed highlighting method. I noticed how the powder adhered to the stone, creating the sensation of a light-colored background. The letters remained in their original darkened state, and stood out quite well against the area surrounding them. Furthermore, I was able to take a splendid photograph of the stone, which would not have been possible otherwise: though legible, the dark letters blended far too well with the rest of the stone for any sort of shadows to appear. Thus, a photograph of an unchalked stone would have looked like a flat rock, with no words.

Once again, cleanup of the young Cubberly gravestone was easily accomplished. The chalk simply washed away with a good scrubbing of water, and no one was the wiser that I had even been there.

On a number of occasions, I have found that the marred condition of a particular stone refused to lend itself to either highlighting or chalking. Often, gaping cracks cut across the face of the marker or small chips pocked the surface. When either of these damaging events occur, mudpacked highlighting and chalking only make the wounds stand out to a greater degree. Hence, the legibility of the epitaph is lost in a mosaic-like effect. After encountering such obstacles on a number of outings, I decided to come up with some other method to highlight the inscription. The result was something which I refer to as tracing.

In easy-to-understand terms, epitaph tracing is a temporary method of shading the writings of a gravestone's inscription. Actually, if you should decide to use this method, you will be reaching toward the opposite end result of chalking: instead of having highlighted the background, you will have colored the letters. Sometimes, particularly if you want to photograph the stone, it is essential to outline or trace each letter individually.

As with the chalking method, I have found that the best means of conducting a tombstone tracing project is to incorporate the use of common white chalk, colored chalk, or soapstone. In this way, you will not damage or deface the marker in any permanent way; once again, the residue left behind can easily be eradicated with a damp cloth, or will simply wash away during the next heavy rainstorm. In any case, you will leave it in the same condition in which you found it.

To trace an inscription, use the dull, rounded point of the chalk instead of the side edge. Now, carefully follow the worn incisions delicately with your finger, following close behind with the chalk. Make certain that you do not miss any of the more obscure cuts in the stone. If you do, an "e" might end up looking like an "o," or a capital "I" might resemble a "T." Obviously, such mistakes can cause real havoc with your transcription, which is something I learned the hard way.

The first time I attempted to use the tracing method to decipher a rather smooth inscription was in Center Cemetery, Paxton, Massachusetts. It was there that I made my crucial mistake. I was in such a hurry to find out what a particular epitaph said that I missed a number of incisions which were barely evident. The end result was a jumbled up message which read:

<pre>
                    llo livod
                    llo wopt
                    llo smilod
                    And diod.
</pre>

Obviously, I was confused by the whole inscription, and decided to try it once again. I washed away the chalk with a damp cloth, and started the entire process again. Meticulously, I rubbed my fingers across the letters, and I soon discovered that I had missed a number of cross incisions. In fact, I was embarassed to realize that the "ll" was actually an "H." Furthermore, every one of the seven "o's" became "e's," and the message eventually became clear to me:

<pre>
                    He lived
                    He wept
                    He smiled
                    And died.
</pre>

Epitaphs to young children, such as the above inscription dedicated to Sidney Ellis, are usually devoid of any conscious humor. More often than not, in fact, the grief of the parents is revealed in a strange way, or simply states all that occurred in the child's life.

Since the above procedures will not suffice for all situations, you may be forced to use other measures to decipher a particular epitaph. Furthermore, you will encounter some inscriptions which you will want to take home with you. If so, photography, which is thoroughly discussed in the next chapter, may be an ideal alternative.

Chapter 9

Tombstone Photography

When my soul hunts range and
rest beyond the great divide -
Just plant me on some strip of
West that's sunny lone and wide.
Let cattle rub my headstone round
and coyote wail their kin.
Let horses come and paw the mound
But do not fence me in.

If you begin to spend a good deal of time seeking out and collecting tombstone literature, you will undoubtedly have a strong desire to organize the epitaphs and carvings that you discover into some type of collection. For that reason, I am briefly going to outline the essential how-to steps of tombstone photography. Keep in mind, however, that I am by no means a professional photographer, though I have learned a great deal about the subject from reading, watching, and participating.

Fortunately for most of you, I will make an avid attempt at staying away from the highly technical aspects in my description of taking good photographs of headstones. Besides, if you approach the hobby of collecting from my point of view, you will soon discover that technicalities and enjoyment don't necessarily mix. In essence, I will simply describe the correct procedures to take in order to make your pictures better than ordinary. Furthermore, I will discuss ideas for taking excellent photographs with the least possible complication and expense.

Before we get down to the basic step-by-step techniques of tombstone photography, I must first outline the essential "tools" of the trade. Hence, the following few pages are intended for those of you who know little, if anything, about taking pictures. Others who have some solid background in the field may, however, want to read on, for I will touch upon a few aspects of photographing headstones in particular.

Just as the stone carver of yesteryear selected his hammer, chisel, and stone carefully before carving, you should choose the correct film for your camera. Film comes in a wide variety of different types for different kinds of results. Most cameras on the market today are adaptable in their ability to use black-and-white or color film which, in turn, produces black-and-white prints, color prints, or color slides. Whenever the weather conditions and the gravestone's etchings are of clear quality, it is generally acceptable to use a "general-purpose" type film. However, whenever lighting conditions are unusually poor, and the stone's carvings or lettering are slightly difficult to see with the naked eye, "special-purpose" films are in order. Due to the fact that these are high-speed films, however, keep in mind that they should only be used with automatic or adjustable cameras.

There are as many types of cameras as there are types of tombstones, and you don't need to purchase an expensive model to take excellent photographs. In fact, when I first began my tombstone photograph collection, it was quite by accident. With my Kodak model camera in hand, I stopped off in a number of small towns throughout the Midwest in search of vanishing American heritage. In Plattsburg, Missouri, I happened upon an elegant, aging courthouse which seemed like an excellent subject for a photo album. While snapping a variety of shots of the building itself, I spotted a curious monument situated on the freshly-cut lawn which read:

David Rice Atchinson
President of the United States for one day.
1807-1886
Lawyer, Statesman and Jurist
United States Senate 1843-1855

Was it possible that a long-lost president was, indeed, memorialized there? I wondered, as I raised my camera and snapped a few haphazard shots. I took the time to do some research at the local library to find the answer. I discovered to my surprise that David Rice Atchinson was president *pro tempore* of the Senate when the term of President Zachary Taylor ended. Due to the fact that that particular day (March 4th) fell on a Sunday, the inaugural ceremony for James K. Polk was delayed until Monday. And, by virtue of his Senate position, Atchinson was, indeed, president of the United States for a few hours.

Anxious to show my friends what I had discovered on the front lawn of the Plattsburg courthouse, I sent the film to a local developing firm near my home. To my disappointment, however, the photograph was overexposed beneath the bright July sunshine. I quickly realized the importance of careful photography. Actually, the camera itself had little to do with my initial failure at tombstone photography. Knowing what you have and understanding precisely how to use what you have, in fact, was the lesson I learned. It is far more important than buying a good deal of expensive equipment.

Basically, cameras can be classified into three types: easy-to-use, automatic, and adjustable. Generally speaking, easy-to-use cameras have few, if any, adjustable knobs, dials, or settings. Furthermore, you can use one to take photos outdoors on sunny days, or you can take flash pictures under overcast conditions. The main thing to keep in mind is that you must maintain a specific distance, or "range," between the tombstone and the camera. And since each easy-to-use camera is designed uniquely from all others, it is absolutely essential that you read your owner's manual to find out precisely what this range is.

Automatic cameras, on the other hand, require slightly more expertise. The portion of the automatic camera that makes it "automatic" is its "exposure-control" mechanism. If you are just starting out on your adventure to become a competent photographer of tombstone inscriptions and carvings, take your camera out to the nearest cemetery for some practice shots. After all, it is important to get a "feel" for sunlight, dimension, focus, and angle if you hope to build an artistic collection.

As you aim the camera and compose your photograph, be aware that the exposure-control mechanism is evaluating the amount of light reflected from the headstone and automatically sets the camera accordingly. Hence, all you need to be concerned with is "telling" the exposure-control mechanism the speed of the film which you are using. The film speed (ASA) is always listed on the film carton or the film instruction sheet, and your owner's manual will assist you in setting the camera's film speed to match it. Don't panic, however, if you are unable to locate this setting mechanism: a number of cameras on the market today possess a notch in the film cartridge, which automatically sets the speed for you as you load it. Once again, see the owner's guide to determine if this is the case with your camera.

Some automatic cameras have what is known as a fixed focus type of lens, which is preset at the factory. This allows you to take quality photographs from an approximate minimum range of four feet up to an almost unlimited distance (or at least as far as the human eye can see). If you have such a lens on your camera, you will always want to get as close as you can, while maintaining a clear and accurate portrait of the stone. Other automatic cameras possess a free-focusing lens, which will allow you to adjust the lens by setting the focusing scale for the distance from the camera to the headstone. This feature will be discussed in-depth in the following paragraphs.

If you should happen to own an adjustable camera, and you are not overly familiar with its operation, you must first over-come your fear of handling and using it. If you are, indeed, "photophobic" because of your inexperience or feelings of inade-quacy around mechanical equipment, you should feel a slight bit of relief from the knowledge that the most complicated cameras on the market today have only three basic settings. They include adjustments for the focus, shutter speed, and lens opening. Allow me the pleasure of introducing you to these mysterious features, which will in turn help you to overcome your apprehension.

Focusing an adjustable camera is carried out in much the same fashion as focusing an automatic model which posesses a free-focusing mechanism: by simply setting the focusing scale for the distance from the camera to the headstone. In fact, some cameras even possess a special range-finder to assist you in focus-ing. If your model does have this range-finding feature, all you need do is turn the focusing ring until two headstone images line up in the camera's viewfinder. When they are lined up, the camera is focused for the correct distance.

Simply put, shutter speed settings on an adjustable camera control the amount of time that outside light will strike the film when exposed. Notice that these various speeds are, more than likely, marked by such numbers as 30, 60, 125, 250, and 500 (although some models have 25, 50, 100, and so on). These numbers actually stand for fractions of seconds, and therefore signify 1/30, 1/60, 1/125, 1/250, and 1/500 of a second. Adjust-ing your camera from one shutter speed to the next larger one lets in half as much light, and moving down in scale lets in twice as much. Shutter speeds which are relatively close together (such as 1/30 and 1/60) produce only slightly different results which are, for all practical purposes, quite difficult to discern.

For most daytime photographs, you'll most likely want to position your shutter speed at 125, or 1/125 of a second. This setting is ideal for pictures on a sunny day. Also, it helps to mini-mize the disastrous effect of camera movement, which, by the way, is the major reason that tombstone photographs are ruined. Don't relax your motionless habits while taking shots, however, for you should still hold your camera as steady as possible.

A camera's lens opening determines the amount of light that reaches the film. Numbers are used to indicate the variations in size of these lens opening settings. These are known as f-numbers, and 2.8, 4, 5.6, 8, 11, 16, and 22 are typical numbers seen on most adjustable cameras. Now, don't let me confuse you, but the *smallest* number on the lens coincides with the *largest* lens opening, and the *largest* lens number coincides with the *smallest* opening. Furthermore, the distance between any specific f-number and its nearest neighbor is referred to as a "stop." Hence, adjusting the opening from f/5.6 to f/4 means that you are opening the lens one stop. As is the case with shutter speed settings, when you move from one lens opening to the next larger one (f/16 to f/11, for example), you are letting in twice as much light.

Now that you understand that the number dials on your camera control the shutter speed and lens opening, you are ready to tackle the job of combining the two for excellent photographs. Basically, there are two simple methods that you can employ to decipher which shutter speed and lens opening to use to reach optimal results.

The easiest way to determine best exposure is to use your film instruction pamphlet. If you open it up, you'll find a detailed exposure table, which outlines shutter speed and lens opening recommendations for outdoor lighting conditions. Normally, this guide will highlight a minimum of four or five basic situations: (1) bright or hazy sun on light sand or snow, (2) bright or hazy sun with distinct shadows, (3) cloudy bright with no shadows, (4) heavy overcast lighting, and (5) open shade (where the stone will actually be shaded from the sun but highlighted by a large area of sky).

For the first three examples above, the pamphlet recommends a shutter speed of 1/125 of a second; however, each requires a different f-stop. Under bright or hazy sun on light sand or snow, f/11 is recommended; beneath bright or hazy sun with distinct shadows, an f/8 setting is best; and for cloudy, bright conditions with no shadows, f/4 is required. For the last two examples described above, the f/4 lens opening is recommended, while the shutter speed should be adjusted to 1/60 of a second.

A second method that you can employ to determine accurate exposure is to employ an exposure meter. While most cameras possess a built-in meter, you can also purchase one that is separate. As with some automatic cameras, you must first "tell" the meter the speed of your film, and then simply follow the manufacturer's recommendations to set the meter. An exposure meter can really come in handy while photographing headstones, since you will in all likelihood encounter a wide range of lighting conditions.

109

Undoubtedly, if you are well-versed in math, you have come to the conclusion that employing numerous combinations of shutter speeds and lens openings will leave you with the same results. Hence, you may be asking yourself: "Why should I bother to learn all the adjustments?" Let me answer your question by simply saying that versatility is the watchword in using your camera equipment to the best of its ability.

Composing wonderful photographs of cemetery headstones is not only a hobby, but an art, and an amateur photographer can quickly become a professional by learning a number of important special techniques. And, first and foremost in your expanding area of expertise is employing concise "depth of field."

Simply put, depth of field is the distance range in which various background objects in your headstone portraits become sharp. For your purpose, you will sustain a greater depth of field if you learn to use a small lens opening (such as f/22). But keep in mind that when you use a small f-stop opening, you should also adjust the shutter speed by the same amount to maintain adequate exposure. Hence, if you move from f/16 to f/22, you should also reset the shutter speed from 1/125 to 1/60.

In photographing epitaphs and artwork on headstones, you can use depth of field to your advantage as a means of controlling your background. If, for example, you desire an out-of-focus backdrop in order to accentuate the stone, you will simply want to enlarge the lens opening (to f/2.8, for example). This will result in a "shallow" depth of field, thus pushing the background out of focus. On the other hand, if you hope to produce a closeup shot with extremely sharp, in-focus background, you can do so by simply employing a smaller lens opening (say an f/16 setting). Once again, it doesn't hurt to dabble with various settings in order to determine your own personal preference.

While using most fixed-focus cameras, you can produce sharp photographs as close as 4 or 5 feet away, and adjustable type cameras often focus well within 2 to 3 feet. While this is close enough for headstones with larger lettering and carvings, it is still too far away for the more intricate details that appear in specific areas of headstones that you may encounter. In a small churchyard cemetery twelve miles north of Bennington, Vermont, I happened upon a monument dedicated to William H. H. Paul. Though there was no carved artwork on the worn marble stone, it did possess an interesting epitaph:

Wm. H. H.
son of Peter M.
& Maria Paul,
died July 11,
1842,
AE 2 y's & 8 d's.
Cropt in the bloom
by deaths arrest
God called me home
He knows what's best.

The epitaph itself was printed with significantly smaller italicized lettering than the names and date, and was made even more difficult to read by the fact that it was clouded over with black staining from natural growth. At the time, I shot the photograph from approximately four feet away without much hesitation and continued my examination of the other nearby stones.

Once again, I had problems when the film was developed. Even though the larger lettering was quite easy to read, the epitaph itself was lost in a sea of shadows. I did not become discouraged, however, with my new-found hobby, for I soon learned that I could move in much closer to a headstone by simply using an inexpensive close-up lens. Your local camera equipment dealer can be of great assistance in selecting exactly what you will need for your particular camera.

While employing a close-up lens, keep in mind that the strength of the lens is determined by its number, which might be 1+, 2+, 3+, and so on. The larger the number, the closer you can move in to photograph a particular headstone. In fact, it is also possible to use a combination of closeup lenses to get even closer. For instance, you might choose to use a 2+ lens and a 3+ lens together while photographing a specific carved etching of a miniature skeletal figure or weaved border. If you do decide to combine them, make certain that the largest numbered lens is placed on your camera first.

Another ingredient to be aware of while using close-up lenses is that each will focus sharply within only a very limited range of a few inches. Therefore, to produce accurate and concise shots, I recommend using lens openings between f/8 and f/22. If you own an automatic camera, this means that you should shoot only under bright sunlight or use a flash. Below is an outline of recommended close-up lenses, along with their individual ranges:

Lens	Range
1+	20 3/8 to 30 3/4 inches
2+	13 3/8 to 19 1/2 inches
3+	10 to 13 inches
4+	8 to 9 7/8 inches
5+	6 1/2 to 7 7/8 inches
6+	5 5/8 to 6 1/2 inches
8+	4 5/8 to 5 1/8 inches
10+	4 to 4 1/4 inches

While using a close-up lens in close proximity to the headstone, note that the viewfinder will not show precisely what will be in the resulting photograph. This is due to the fact that the viewfinder is situated slightly higher than the lens. This phenomenon is known as a parallax view, and can be compensated for by tipping the camera ever so slightly in the direction of the viewfinder after you have composed your picture. In fact, the closer you move toward the headstone, the more you need to tip the camera upward in order to capture the picture you first saw in the viewfinder. If you fail to tip the camera to compensate, the result will be that the headstone will appear slightly higher on the print.

If you are a poor judge of distance, it is quite easy to make a device that will measure the distance to the headstone and show you precisely what will be included in your final picture. First, study the instruction sheet that came with your close up lens, which details the range, width of the camera field, and focus setting for that particular lens. Next, cut a piece of cardboard that is the exact dimensions of these measurements, using the camera range for length and the camera field for width. Finally, draw a dark, black line down the center of the cardboard's length.

To measure for precise distance from the headstone, hold the cardboard out from your camera directly in front of the center of the close-up lens. Through the viewfinder, line up the black line of the cardboard with the center of what you hope to capture on film. Next, align the portion of the stone to be photographed so that it barely touches the end of the card and is positioned within the card's width. Now, holding the camera totally steady, simply drop the card and squeeze the shutter release gently.

Another drawback with close-up shots is the ever-disruptive problem with ample lighting. For the most part, the best rule to follow in the production of sound headstone photography is to shoot close-ups beneath bright sunshine. Unfortunately, however, Mother Nature, combined with the intrusive atmosphere of a great many tree-shaded cemeteries, are not always accommodating. Therefore, you may need to create the illusion of bright sunlight.

Since sunlight will produce an ever-changing combination of shadows and light, you should first check your headstone to make certain that it is not covered by patches of shade. If it is, my best advice would be to wait until sunlight prevails. Often, this is not possible. If you find yourself in such a situation, don't despair. You can simply use a large sheet of white paper or aluminum foil to reflect sunlight onto the stone. If you choose this makeshift technique, however, make sure that you angle the paper or foil reflector at a 45-degree angle to the stone. This will produce shadows in the stone's crevices, which are essential in highlighting epitaphs and intricate carvings.

You can also employ an on-camera flash for close-up photography in a cemetery on overcast days or beneath heavy shadows. However, since the amount of artificial light produced by a flash will be too much at such a close range, you must first cut down the amount of light. Otherwise, the photograph will be overexposed. The easiest way to accomplish this is to drape a white, cotton cloth over the flash reflector or cube, thus filtering out a certain degree of light. If you should happen to own a fixed-focus camera, use the chart below in accessing the number of layers of cotton cloth to use:

Headstone Distance	Layers of Cloth
6 inches	4 layers
12 inches	3 layers
18 inches	2 layers
24 inches	2 layers
30 inches	1 layer
36 inches	1 layer

This chart can also be adequately employed with an adjustable camera if your lens setting is positioned at f/11.

Employing a flash off the camera (which attaches to your camera with an extension cord) will assist you in creating the appearance of angled light and shadow - ingredients which are necessary for capturing dimension within the nooks and crannies of a stone's artwork. Holding the flash at arm's length requires a bit of manual dexterity, since you will be forced to operate the camera with one hand while you hold the flash with the other. The easiest solution to this "juggling act" that I have found is to ask a friend to hold the flash while you take the photograph.

113

If you find that your flash cord isn't long enough to create the correct angle of shadow, your photo dealer can supply you with an inexpensive extension. However, whatever you use, keep in mind that you should figure your exposure on the distance from flash to the headstone, rather than camera to headstone. When using a close-up lens, you should also keep in mind that it is virtually impossible to bring the background of your photograph into perfect focus. However, an out-of-focus background will enhance your finished artwork, offering an unobtrusive rainbow of blurred color that will complement the outline of the headstone.

If, on the other hand, you do not want this blurred effect in your photographs, you can produce shots with plain dark or single-colored backdrops. To accomplish this, simply position a black or dull-finished colored paper behind the headstone. These artificial backgrounds can be secured at any art supply outlet, and will work to outline the headstone in sharp contrast. You should stay away from grays, greens, and blue-tone paper, since these are commonly the color combinations of 17th- and 18th-century headstones. Remember: contrast, not similarity, is needed in order to "frame" your portraits.

There is one other important aspect of photography to remember when taking shots of headstone artwork. Often a particular marker can be arranged in such a manner that you might want to position a point of special interest on the headstone so that it is slightly off-center on the photograph. I discovered just such a stone in Evergreen Cemetery, Central Village, Connecticut. On one side of the four-sided shaft was carved the following tribute:

Rosa
My first Jersey Cow
Record 2 lbs. 15 ozs. Butter
From 18 qts. 1 day milk.

On this particular occasion, I had the urge to capture Rosa's image, which was carved neatly above the inscription, as well as what I found etched into an adjacent side - a grand carving of a violin crossed by a bow. It commemorated Gurdon Cady, a local farmer and leader of a late 19th century dance orchestra. Below the bow were the following words:

All ready, Mr. Cady.

Local legend has it that whenever the floor manager had paired couples for a square dance, he would turn to Cady and say those very words.

In composing this intriguing combination through my viewfinder, I employed a tried-and-true method for slightly off-center photography. First, I stood directly in front of the angle separating the two adjacent sides, making sure that both carvings (as well as their inscriptions) were clearly discernable. Then, I mentally divided the composition into thirds, both vertically and horizontally, which made a checkerboard of nine equal parts. Next, I positioned Rosa's image on one of the four places where the lines intersected. Finally, I took the picture at a 45 degree angle, capturing both scenes completely, along with a slanted image of their accompanying epitaphs.

Well, there you have it: a beginner's course in headstone photography. Now you are fairly well-equipped to visit the world of your long-lost ancestors and return home with a small piece of the past. If you do not, however, wish to pursue the art of photography, you would be well-advised to continue reading. There are other methods to choose from for the avid collector of headstone carvings and literature.

Chapter 10

Tombstone Rubbings & Dabbings

Major Allen Hurst
Son of
John & Elizabeth Thompson
Hurst
March 4, 1810 Tazwell Co. Va.
May 26, 1873.
First Circuit Court Clerk
Of Union Co.
During Reconstruction
Days Robbed by the Carpet
Baggers of 4000 Acres
Of Land.
60 Odd Years Later T.V.A.
Confiscated Several
Thousand Acres of Mineral
Land Left to his Grand
Children
Gone With the Wind.

Numerous hobbyists who take the time to read and enjoy tombstone literature and sculpted carvings will not be satisfied to simply search out and photograph those inscriptions and etchings that seem curious or quaint. This also holds true for many genealogists currently seeking some added credibility for their family heritage. Instead, these would-be cemetery researchers desire a more permanent memento of their new-found pastime; some evidence, as it were, that they might hold on to for future posterity. The answer to their dilemma seems to lie in the gathering of original tombstone inscriptions and their accompanying artwork on paper.

The practice of tombstone transfer is currently on the rise throughout America, but few well-researched sources are available that offer step-by-step instructions on what should be done to perfect such skills.

Perhaps the best method available for any researcher to permanently secure the strong graphic qualities and unique inscriptions on aging tombstones is a technique referred to as gravestone rubbing. Though there are a variety of ways to conduct this type of artwork, I will describe the most satisfactory method in terms of cost-efficiency, enjoyment, reproduction, and simplicity.

In easy to understand terms, a rubbing is a quick method often used by hobbyists to reproduce the surface of an object. Most of us participated in such activities as children when we placed an object, such as a coin or leaf, beneath a piece of paper. Then, using the dulled edge of a pencil or crayon, we rubbed the surface of the object through the paper. Almost like magic, the contours began to come through, and we were delighted with our ingenuity.

As I grew up, I discovered that there was a wide array of common household items which I could use to make simple rubbings. They included rough-cut wood and sandpaper from my father's workshop, the raised floral wallpaper of our dining room, my mother's antique lace doilies, and even the aging book bindings of our family's treasured leatherbound classics. Soon, I was making rubbings of everything that I could lay my hands on, and I habitually kept my rubbing supplies with me wherever I went. Eventually, during a family vacation through the New Orleans, Louisiana area I happened upon an interesting inscription in one of the local cemeteries, which read:

> He did acts of kindness
> and charity, as stealthily
> as some men commit crimes.

Intrigued by the words, I quickly set about making a pencil rubbing of the stone; which, incidentally, came out looking like a scribbled mess, the result of a rough-cut stone. I knew then as I know now that there is a great deal of patience and ingenuity required when pursuing the hobby of tombstone rubbing. Hopefully, I will be able to share a bit of my hard-earned expertise in the next few pages.

Before driving out to your local cemetery to begin your collection in "gung-ho" style, you should first purchase large sheets, pads, or rolls of paper from a nearby office supply or art retail store. While you are there, you should also shop around for a box of soft lead drafting pencils, colored chalk, artists' charcoal, and black lumber-marking wax crayons (the type that shippers use when marking cardboard or wooden packing crates). Any of these can be used to make an adequate rubbing, and your choice will depend upon the type of stone you encounter and your preference in their varied results. This will be discussed in greater detail later.

From years of experience, I have found that ordinary postal wrapping paper, drafting paper, table cloth paper which is rolled smooth, or 20-weight bond typing or copy paper is sufficient. Your very best choice, however, is any wide roll of paper that contains a minimum of 25% cotton fiber content, for its texture depicts the finished rubbing neatly, it resists smudging, and it holds up to more than a slight amount of abuse.

Whichever type of paper you choose, make sure that it possesses a bit of body, or thickness. Also, be aware that there are specific varieties to avoid all together. For example, onionskin paper will cause you definite problems. This also holds true for anything that claims to be "erasable bond" paper. Each of these is far too thin to stand up to the rough surface of many tombstones, and may tend to wrinkle, puncture, and tear with the slightest bit of pressure. Furthermore, they absorb headstone dirt and skin oil quite easily, and will inevitably smear and smudge while you are making your rubbing.

After you have purchased your paper and rubbing utensils, make sure to buy two or three rolls of ordinary 1/2- or 1-inch masking tape. You'll be using this to hold your paper in place over the stone's face to ensure that it does not move around while you work; even the slightest amount of shifting will result in a blurring of the design.

Before going any further, you should first test the compatibility of the paper with the tape. To do so, cut off a small length of paper (a few inches should do it) and press a strip of the masking tape along the paper's outermost edge. After leaving it in place for fifteen to twenty minutes (the amount of time you'll later need to complete a rubbing), carefully peel the tape back, trying not to tear the paper in the process. If they separate quite easily, you should not have a problem removing the tape from a future finished rubbing. If they don't come apart readily, however, you should investigate other easy-to-remove varieties. There are a number of these available from retailers, arts and crafts shops, and office supply stores.

Now it is time to go out to your local cemetery to work on your first project. After you have completed your tombstone salvage work (see chapter 8 for further details), you will be ready to begin the other preparatory processes. Using an ordinary measuring tape, record the precise dimensions of the stone's face. Make certain to include not only the personal data and epitaph, but also any interesting figure carvings you might wish to preserve. Now, if at all possible, cut off a length of paper that will easily cover the entire face of the tombstone with some left over. It is best not to place separate sheets together in a piecemeal fashion, since you might have a problem keeping the paper in place while making the actual rubbing. Besides, when separation lines between sheets show on the finished artwork, the end result looks far less professional.

Now, using an ordinary pair of scissors, trim the paper down to size, making certain to leave an extra two or three inches of excess border along all edges. This will provide you with a workable area that can be trimmed away later, and will give you the ability to frame your completed rubbing, much like a painter frames an oil canvas.

If after you have finished trimming your paper you decide that you only wish to make a rubbing of a small portion of the stone, fold the edges so that you have approximately 1/2-inch of overlapped double-edging. Although this step is not absolutely necessary, it will give you added protection against tearing and wrinkling, which most often occurs around the thin edges when you remove the securement tape. Now, using the 1/2- or 1-inch masking tape, attach your paper securely over the area you wish to copy, leaving only four or five inches of space between each length of tape. Make certain that your paper is positioned perfectly flat against the stone, and that there are no "waves" to contend with - this, too, will allow the paper to move around.

On the other hand, if you have decided to make a rubbing of the entire face of the stone, skip the above step and position the paper in such a way that the two-inch to three-inch paper excess extends beyond the stone's outermost edges. Bend the excess at the edges of the stone so that they wrap around the sides and top, much like you would wrap a boxed Christmas gift. Using this method, you will be able to keep the paper more stable while you are rubbing. To make absolutely certain that it does not slip and slide, use your masking tape to attach it securely to the sides (not the face) of the stone.

Under no circumstances should you use what I call the double sticky-side taping method to hold your paper in place. In essence, this involves folding a length of tape back over itself, placing the two ends together in such a way that both front and back have sticky sides facing out. Typically, this double sticky-side tape is then placed on the back side of the paper so that it does not show. There are two major problems with this, however: (1) the paper will not be held firmly in place, and (2) the outline of the tape will show up on the front surface of the rubbing. There is no need for incorporating the double sticky-side taping method anyway, since it doesn't really matter whether or not the tape shows while you work - you will simply be removing and discarding it later.

Keep in mind that a wide variety of other materials are quite suitable for making rubbings. Instead of paper, for example, I have tried several different types of cloth, including cotton, silk, broadcloth, and even old bed sheets and pillow cases. Obviously, the thicker the material, the more apt you will be to lose some of the stone's intricately carved detail. Still, it is essential to hold the material firmly in place as you rub, for fabric of any sort is inclined to move and stretch, which may distort the image.

If you do decide to employ cloth in your rubbings, make sure to use wax crayon as your marking material - the other varieties will not work as efficiently. Furthermore, though an open-knit or coarse material will provide some interesting textured backgrounds for your finished rubbing, they will further subtract from its clarity of detail. Finally, to prevent smearing and smudging on cloth once you have completed your project, simply iron the reverse side of the material.

If you are using paper which has already been firmly put in place, it will be time to decide whether to use a soft lead pencil, colored chalk, artists' charcoal, or lumber-marking wax crayon. This, as I indicated before, depends on two considerations: (1) what type of stone you are working with, and (2) what you want your finished artwork to look like.

The character, or essence, of your rubbing will depend largely on the surface of the stone. Sandstone, which possesses the coarsest texture of all early-day markers, has proven to be a major problem for people making tombstone rubbings. If this happens to be what you are working with, you will not want to use the soft lead pencil. If you do, the rubbing will come out looking like a pitted mess, and the paper will have a tendency to puncture when you least expect it. Instead, with sandstone and other coarse surfaces, choose the colored chalk, charcoal, or wax crayons for your graphic work.

If on the other hand you are working with schist or marble, the soft lead pencil is the ideal rubbing utensil. The smoother the surface, the more difficult it is to create a satisfactory rubbing with chalk and, particularly, wax crayons. Keep in mind that if you are using a soft-lead pencil on this type of surface, you must rub with an even-pressured stroke. Furthermore, such rubbings may take two or three attempts, at least until you get the hang of it.

Perhaps, of all stone surfaces, slate yields the greatest contrast in image, and will prove to be the most satisfactory. This is due in large part to its fine, even grain, and resistance to cracking. For this type of surface, you can choose to use any of the markers. All possess the ability to produce not only an adequate, but an excellent finished product. In fact, you may decide to do what I have done on a number of occasions: make a number of rubbings of the same stone, using a variety of different materials. Such was the case with a particularly intriguing headstone which I discovered in the Ancient Burying Ground, Hartford, Connecticut:

Here lyeth the body of Mr. David Gardiner
of Gardiner's Island deceased July 10, 1689
in the fifty-fourth year of his age.
Well-sick-dead in one hour's space.
Engrave the remembrance of Death on thine heart
When as thow dost see how swiftly hours depart.
Born at Saybrook April 29, 1636
The first white child born in Connecticut.

Over time, you will undoubtedly develop a preference in rubbing utensils. Personally, I prefer the sheer, delicate look of chalk, aside from the fact that color adds an aesthetic touch. Others, however, may favor the stark black-and-white contrast that results from using charcoal. On the other hand, anyone who is partial to the smooth stroke of pencil sketches may prefer the soft lead design, since it shows every intricate shadow. And, though the wax crayon is my least favorite, it seems easier to work with and will stand up better to abuse. Still, the choice is yours, for each appeals to a different type of collector.

You are now ready to make the actual rubbing of the stone. Using the broad edge of the pencil, chalk, charcoal, or crayon, rub the entire surface of the paper lightly in an even back-and-forth motion. For now, you are not attempting to pick up every single detail of the stone, just to establish the overall pattern. Make certain as you work that you do not use a great deal of pressure. After all, you don't want your artistic creation to be filled with unsightly puncture wounds. Gradually, if done correctly, the entire inscription will be transferred from the stone to the paper.

Now, step back and take stock of your work. Notice that the portion of the stone that comes in contact with the underside of the paper has been recorded in darker coloration. At the same time, that part that is recessed, or incised, is represented by white, or uncolored, patterns. This contrast may seem amazing to a first-time collector.

After you have completed this preliminary effort, you will need to go over the entire rubbing a second time. Using a bit more pressure, slowly work your pencil, chalk, charcoal, or crayon in from the edges that separate the surface area of the stone from the depressed background. When done with care, your rubbing will gradually become more concise, exhibiting every minute detail.

It is now time to gently remove the masking tape holding your masterpiece in place, taking ample care not to tear or wrinkle the corners of the paper in the process. If this should happen in spite of your precautions, however, do not be overly concerned; this is precisely why you left extra paper around the edges. Special care should also be taken not to brush up against or touch the surface of your work; clothing causes smudging, and oily fingers tend to make the finished product somewhat illegible.

Monumental brasses are often found in a number of old cemeteries and churches. The beginning hobbyist should be aware that making a rubbing of an epitaph etched into this delicate material requires a totally different process. *Never, under any circumstances, follow the instructions described above while working with engraved brass.* More on this a bit later.

In order to protect your rubbing from the damage that handling can inflict, you'll want to give it a light coating with an ordinary can of aerosol hair spray, which will act as a temporary non-smearing agent until you get your artwork safely home. The only time that this is not recommended, however, is on a windy day. Not only will the spray fly in every direction except toward its intended destination, but it will tend to coagulate into clots on the surface of your rubbing. Besides, minute dust and sand particles may also be blowing about in the air, and these do not mix well with sticky hair spray.

To proceed, lay your rubbing face-up on a flat surface with ample layers of newspaper underneath. After shaking the can of hair spray for several seconds, test the spraying action to make certain that the nozzle is not clogged before taking aim. If it seems to be flowing evenly, hold the nozzle 4 to 10 inches from the rubbing's surface. Depress the button fully, spraying with long, smooth, parallel strokes. In order to avoid leaving untreated areas, make sure that you overlap approximately 1/2 of each preceding stroke as you spray. Finally, allow several minutes drying time before you move the rubbing.

If you want to make absolutely certain that your artistic endeavors will last indefinitely, there are a number of other protective measures that might be taken. For instance, you might invest some extra money in acid-free paper and spray fixative intended for artists' use. For a minimal cost, a commercial product can be

123

used instead of (or even over) the hair spray coating. One example is known as Depthane, a water-resistant clear satin polyurethane spray. It contains no dangerous fluorocarbons, lead, or benzene, and it is non-toxic when dry. Furthermore, you can switch from standard spray to a much thinner "fanspray" by simply rotating the valve tip 1/4 of a turn. However, please be advised that a much longer drying time (approximately six hours) is needed, and that the entire procedure should be done twice for best results.

Now that you have completed your initial rubbing, take stock of your work. Do not be upset if all has not gone well, for in this business of making tombstone rubbings practice does, indeed, make perfect. Simply review the common faults that might lead to an imperfect product:

(1) Blurred Image or Lettering: Once again, this is usually caused by allowing the paper to move while rubbing. Remember - always make absolutely certain that the paper is secured firmly in place by masking tape. Helpful Hint - try working from the top of the stone down toward the bottom and rub only a small area at a time.

(2) Smudging: This may be caused by rubbing up against your finished product or touching the rubbing with oily hands. Remember - purchase a fixative spray to "fix" the completed project. Helpful Hint - a product known as an Astral Stick is reputed to be the best rubbing utensil on the market if you wish to avoid smudging.

(3) Paper Tearing: Usually, this is the result of using paper that is too thin. Remember - rub very lightly with the edge of your marking utensil to avoid any sharp edges which protrude from the stone. Helpful Hint - rub your hand lightly over the stone before putting the paper in place to feel for any rough edges.

Placing a protective plastic covering over your finished rubbing is important; I will discuss how to go about this in greater detail later in this chapter. If done correctly, your rubbings will last indefinitely. I still have one particular eight year old rubbing hanging in my living room, which declares:

Lord I commit my soul to thee
Accept the sacred trust
Receive this nobler part of me
And watch my sleeping dust.

Anyone who is an avid collector of tombstone rubbings should be aware that there are a number of ways to improvise on your creations. If you are the type, for example, who prefers using dark-colored wax crayons on white paper, you might try employing white wax on dark paper. In essence, this provides a finished product that looks something like a "negative" of the normal rubbing.

Those of you who are somewhat adventurous may even decide to take this one step further by creating a rubbing using white wax crayon on white paper. Although initially this may sound foolhardy, there is one added step which will offer a much different result. The entire process is known as the resist rubbing method.

As always, place the wide paper over the entire face, fold it tightly around the stone's sides, and attach it firmly in place with masking tape. Next, carefully rub the white wax crayon over the inscription and artwork. After you have removed the half-finished rubbing, separate the tape from the paper, take it home, and lay it on a flat surface over some old newspapers. Now, using a soft brush, paint over the entire surface of your rubbing with ink or water color paints. As you progress, maintain light, even movements of the brush, making certain that you paint in the same direction with each stroke. Soon, you will see that the ink or paint will soak into the paper, but not the wax, leaving behind a white image. Allow ample time for drying before spraying with any type of fixative.

If you are, in fact, working with paints and waxes, beware of the dreaded "paint obliteration." Normally, painting ink or water colors over a wax crayon rubbing will fill in the background of your masterpiece. However, you may find that the wax resists showing through the paint. To overcome this problem, simply make certain that the wax crayon is applied thickly, while the ink or paint should be a thin coating.

If you are truly into innovative rubbings, you may choose to use a wide variety of colored crayons in a single rubbing. Use gold, for example, to highlight the carved edging of a stone, and silver for the epitaph itself. After you have completed the rubbing, lay it on a smooth, flat surface and polish it with a clean cotton cloth. This step will produce the added effect of a shiny surface. Instead of polishing, you can also employ a variety of metallic sticks as rubbing utensils, which are available at most art and craft shops. They will produce a dazzling effect when used individually or jointly. In either scenario above, a dark colored paper is particularly impressive as a background.

If you should happen to run across a tombstone which is particularly worn - one in which the carving is so shallow that it will not offer sufficient detail - there is another technique that you might try. Known as tombstone dabbing, it is well worth your while if no other method works, which was the case with a hard-to-read headstone that I found in Mill River, Massachusetts:

Polly Rhoades
Died Sept. 7, 1855:
Aged 86 Yr's 5 Mo's
& 3 d's.
Being the widow of 5 husbands.
1st David Rockwell,
2nd Capt. Alpheus Underwood,
3rd Dea. Amos Langdon,
4th Hezekiah G. Butler,
5th James T. Rhoades.

Actually, the dabbing method is quite easy to employ. First, fashion a dabber by wrapping a piece of chamois leather around a small ball of cotton wool, tying it in place. (Cotton wool is raw cotton; processed cotton does not work as well, since it tends to fall apart.) Next, mix an ample amount of graphite or powdered pencil lead with several drops of olive or linseed oil, working it into paste-like consistency. It is best to do this mixing in an empty plastic butter dish, or on the flat side of a piece of wood.

After you have mixed the ingredients thoroughly, cover the face of the tombstone with a sheet of tissue wrapping-paper or any other thin variety that you can find. Now, while holding it in place with masking tape, dab a bit of the graphite mixture onto the paper with your homemade dabber. Continue this process, avoiding any rubbing motion, until the entire inscription or image comes through. Though this procedure can take a considerable amount of time and effort, it will pick up detail that might have otherwise been passed over. Now, carefully remove the tape from the stone and trim it away from the tissue with a pair of scissors. Finally, spray the "dabbing" with fixative to prevent smudging.

As I have already stated, engraved brass monuments - some nearly 600 years old - can be easily damaged by an unskilled hobbyist. They are often produced from very thin sheets, and exhibit figures, coats of arms, and epitaphs. Furthermore, they are usually laid into a stone slab, which is not always the most stable foundation. For this reason, it is important that you not only secure permission from church officials before pursuing your hobby, but you must purchase different materials.

First, you should find a product known as heelball, which is a mixture of wax and lampblack, used for blackening the heels and edges of the soles of shoes. The most likely source for this is any shoe repair shop or leathercraft store. However, if you are unable to find it, don't despair, for Astral sticks (mentioned earlier) can also be used as a rubbing utensil. For the most part, these sticks are specifically produced for the creation of brass rubbings, and they are smudge-resistant. As always, bring along masking tape and scissors, as well as a clean cotton cloth.

Before you take any of the normal preparatory steps mentioned earlier, it is absolutely essential that you clean the surface of the brass with your cloth. Take your time, and be sure to remove any loose grit or dust which may tear your paper or, more importantly, scratch the brass.

Now, lay the cut paper over the entire face of the brass plate so that it overflows all edges, and then secure it tightly with masking tape. Now, using your index finger and clean cloth, locate the edge of the brass and press tightly around the edge to impress an outline. This step will help to prevent any accidental rubbing over the edge, which may tend to tear your paper. Next, start rubbing at the top of the plate, working slowly toward the bottom. If you are using the heelball you must press fairly hard if you hope to obtain a dark, even effect. When you have completed the rubbing itself, gently brush away any loose flakes of heelball left behind. Finally, after removing the mounted paper and masking tape, gently polish the rubbing with your cloth. It is now ready to be finished.

At times, if you should have the good fortune to discover an epitaph that might in all likelihood become a treasured family heirloom, take the time to carefully preserve it. One suggestion is to cover it, both front and back, with a layer of plastic. For home use, a roll of ordinary clear contact paper will do a relatively fine job. Most commercial brands of this product are sold in rolls wide enough to cover the majority of epitaph rubbings.

It is advised that you try this technique on a blank piece of paper before tackling the "real McCoy," since it takes a bit of practice to reach perfection. After you feel that you have the hang of it, cut a piece of contact paper large enough to cover one side of your rubbing, with enough excess left over for trimming. Carefully peel back the protective backing from the contact paper, laying it sticky-side up on the flat surface of a table. Make certain that the plastic is not wrinkled, folded, or wavy.

Next, place your rubbing face down on the contact paper, starting from one corner and working your way back toward the opposite corner diagonally as you press down. Proceed with extra caution, making certain that your rubbing is perfectly smooth against the plastic. If you should accidentally get a wrinkle or fold in your rubbing, or leave an air pocket in between, you will have ruined your artwork. If all goes well, repeat the entire process and cover the back side of your rubbing. Finally, using a pair of scissors or, better yet, a paper cutter, trim away the excess edges.

A second method used to seal a rubbing is to employ a thermal fax machine, although most commercial makes will only accomidate an 8 1/2 by 11-inch sheet of paper. Many public and university libraries, schools, and office supply rental stores have just such a machine available to the public for a small fee. Using thin sheets of clear plastic to sandwich your artwork, the step-by-step process is quite easy to follow.

First, set the dial of the thermal fax processor in the middle range, which will provide an ample amount of heat. Then, position the rubbing between two sheets of plastic, making certain that all surface area is completely covered. Holding them together firmly, push the entire package into the fax carrying slot, which is normally positioned at the front of the machine. Instantly, the covered rubbing will be fed through the thermal processor and emerge from a second slot. Finally, simply trim away the extra plastic.

If you are at all nervous about risking the application of contact paper with your tombstone rubbing, you may instead let a professional perform the job. Once again, many schools, public libraries, and university libraries will have a laminating machine at their disposal, although they do not ordinarily have them available for public projects. Instead your best bet would be to go to an area media center or retail copy store, where they can perform the service for you. There will be no need to personally deal with sticky plastic when you go this route, for your rubbing will simply be fed through a commercial machine for processing. Within minutes, a thicker grade of plastic will be literally melted (both front and back) over your artwork, creating a permanent seal.

Not only will this assure you of a virtual lifetime of protection, it will keep the paper from turning brown with age. Finally, I have also been known to place the plastic covered rubbing under glass, frame it with rustic wood, and hang it on a vacant wall in my home. In that way, it becomes an instant conversation item for both friends and family alike.

Instead of framing your finished brass rubbing under glass or beneath a protective coating of clear plastic shelving paper, you may want to try a much different approach. Using a long length of bamboo or dowelling material, cut two pieces that are slightly longer than the width of your rubbing. Laying your rubbing out flat, roll the top end of the paper twice around the rod and fix it into position with a strong glue. Repeat this process on the lower end of your rubbing. Finally, knot a length of colored cord or heavy string to each exposed end of the top rod, thus making a hanger for your rubbing.

Tombstone rubbing can be as easy or complicated as you make it, and can provide numerous rewards of epitaphs and artwork which have long thought to have been "lost." Yet if you want a collecting method that is still more obscure to hobbyists, why not try foiling, which is discussed thoroughly in the upcoming chapter.

Chapter 11

Tombstone Foiling

In Memory
of
Mary Heathman Smith
Lovingly known as Granny Smith
Born in England January 21, 1818 where she
was trained in a maternity hospital. She
came to Utah in 1862. As doctor, surgeon,
midwife and nurse, for thirty years, in storm
or sunshine, during the bleakest winter,
or the darkest night, with little or no
remuneration, she attended the people of
Ogden Valley with a courage and faith-
fullness unexcelled. In addition to rearing
her own family of nine, under her skill and
attention she brought into the world
more than 1500 babies. She died at
Huntsville, Utah, December 15, 1895.

A book on the subject of collecting and preserving tombstone epitaphs and art would not be complete if we did not discuss
the process of creating three-dimensional rubbings. In ancient
civilizations, inscriptions chiseled into stone helped to convey a
good deal of knowledge for future generations. Still, despite all of
his dedicated efforts, a stone carver was only able to produce a
single image. In contrast, the method that we are about to discuss
will serve to create mirrored replicas of words and portraits over
and over again, leaving the collector with many copies. The gravestones of your ancestors can be, if you choose, a foundation for a
little-known type of duplication known as foiling.

Incorporating the foiling method into gravestone duplication goes beyond the limitation of two-dimensional pencil, chalk,
or wax rubbings. Not only can it transfer an actual stone texture

to a flat surface, but it reproduces a relief into a clear three-dimensional representation of that relief. The resulting artistic qualities are so striking, at times, that a viewer will be tempted to examine it more closely to see if it is, indeed, the real thing.

Amid the cloud-covered sky that shades a somber grave-yard, a practitioner of the foiling method may be seen making his or her way down the winding pathway through the Old Cemetery in Bennington, Vermont. Pausing alongside the grave of the Reverend Jedediah Dewey, who died in 1778 at the age of 65, he or she may view a macabre invitation left behind for the sake of posterity:

> Of comfort no man speak! Let's talk of
> graves and worms and epitaphs. Make
> dust our paper, and with rainy eyes,
> write sorrow on the bosom of the earth!

The inscription, now more than 200 years old, reminds the collector that stone carvings are only temporary: a mere shadow that may fade with the rising sun.

One thought must have occurred to the man responsible for carving this unique memory into stone: that one day it would weather, erode, and eventually vanish. If only the carved tombstones could somehow be duplicated and preserved, it would mean that these precious thoughts would never fade.

The headstones themselves, however, due to their very nature, presented a stumbling block. In the past, even when a type of lampblack ink was indeed applied to the face of a tombstone, and then a piece of ordinary mulberry-bark paper was pressed against the surface, the end result was disastrous. No doubt, this method did indeed reproduce a printed black copy, with the white characters clearly prominent. Yet clarity stopped there, for each individual printed character appeared in reverse. And since no one seemed to have the solution to the riddle of reverse print, centuries passed without a clear answer.

Eventually, however, there came a historian who had found the solution. While onlookers gathered around a single headstone, he submerged a sheet of paper in a tub of water until it had soaked through. Next he laid the dripping result over the face of the stone. With a stiff-bristled brush, he then pressed the thin paper down firmly into each incision. Finally, he dipped a silk cloth into ink and rubbed it lightly over the entire face.

When the collector pulled the completed project from the surface of the stone, it exhibited the words of the text, highlighted by the ink. As if by some mystical process, the lyrical writing appeared in white against the blackened background. He held it aloft for all to read.

In all actuality, the origin of stone rubbing, or more specifically "ink dabbing," has been obscured by history, though it may indeed have happened as described above. Still, from what has been recorded from ancient Chinese writings, this sort of process most likely originated in the Orient in some similar fashion more than 1,000 years ago.

Evidence indicates that the Chinese also experimented with printing directly from page-sized wooden blocks, upon which writings had been carefully carved in reverse. Much later, artisans realized the advantage of reproducing artwork from gravestones. And today, after decades of research, we have come to develop the process of foiling.

For the modern day tombstone foiler, ordinary kitchen aluminum foil may prove too thin for some rubbings. This is due in large part to the fact that a few inscriptions and artist's adaptations are far too deep, and the results will be that the foil will pucture and tear. Such was the case of an epitaph which I found in the long forgotten burial site of the Estelle family, near Lakewood, New Jersey:

Death did to me
Short warning give,
Therefore, be careful
How you live.
My weeping friends
I leave behind -
I had not time
To speak my mind.

In the event that regular kitchen foil is too thin for your project, thicker aluminum foils can be purchased from artist supply outlets, such as Stafford-Reeves, Inc., located at 626 Greenwich Street in New York City, or Reeves and Sons Ltd, 13 Charing Cross Road, London, England. If you do not, however, desire to search for this stronger material, disposable foil pans (the type used to bake turkeys for Thanksgiving) are an ideal substitute for the thinner grocery store variety. From my own experience, however, conventional kitchen foil, rather than the heavy-duty or quilted brand, seems to work the best. Yet, this is only true if you take on a tombstone foiling project with adequate care and patience. In any event, when you have secured both types (just in case), go out to your nearby cemetery and try your skill.

Before you begin, it is absolutely necessary to understand that a foiler should *never* work with inscriptions etched into brass. This may permanently scratch and mar the brass plate. Furthermore, you should come equipped with a variety of tools: one- or two-inch masking tape, sharp scissors, a large supply of wooden popcicle sticks or a nailbrush, and an old toothbrush. Once again, you should take along all of your headstone excavating and cleaning utensils, including brushes, buckets, trowel, spade, handsaw, and rags. After preparing the stone (as outlined in chapter 8), you will be ready to begin making your initial foiled print.

Prior to covering the headstone over with foil, however, you should first study the intricate details which you hope to capture. Notice the curves and straight lines, and how they blend together into a complete mosiac of artwork. Rub your hand across the surface of the stone, feeling the texture and impressions. Study and learn what you are about to reproduce. When completed, your foil portrait should be an exact copy of the original.

Anyone who is contemplating the creation of a three-dimensional tombstone form should be well-versed in the types of carvings that may be encountered. Basically, there are two varieties: raised-carving and engraving.

Raised-carving on stone is formed so that the actual surface stands out in high relief. In the case of lettering, each individual character was fashioned by situating it on its own little pedestal. Scenes are similarly formed, carved in such a way that the entire portrait is raised slightly above the stone base. Once covered with foil, this raised carving comes in contact with the foil, thus allowing you to depress the background areas.

In working with such a stone in Hingham, Massachusetts, dated 1783, I imagined that such intricate detailing must have taken weeks, or even months, to complete. Proudly, the inscription declared:

Here lies the Remains
of
Capt. Samuel Linclon
and his two wives,
Fanna and Mary.

Painstakingly foiling the rounded top portion of the stone, recessed curved lines in the shapes of feathers began to appear around a concave half-mooned border. Just below, the three faces of the deceased family began to come out in a pyramid fashion, with the gentleman at the apex and the two wives a bit lower. Around each face was inscribed a much larger half-moon, with a bottom straight edge cutting across the neck of each portrait and the ourtermost curved edge highlighted by a zig-zag outline. Perhaps most intriguing of all, however, were the somber facial expressions of the Captain and his two wives, for each stony countenance emmitted a understanding that, despite the marital arrangement, everything was purely prim and proper in the Linclon [sic] household.

Perhaps easier to work with, yet far less typical of 18th- and 19th-century tombstones, is the engraved surface. In past generations, a few stone carvers did not incorporate a raised line. Instead, they cut realistic images into the face of the marker with a sharpened tool known as a graver. They then wiped the surface clean and dry, and polished the entire scene. When pressure is applied to foil covering this type of surface, a relief design will gradually appear, with the portrait itself actually being depressed.

After you have memorized the complete portrait in your mind's eye, measure the tombstone's face accurately, and trim a larger-than-needed length of foil. Lay the foil over the entire face of the stone, and gently bend it around the edges of the marker. Next, as with making a rubbing, fix the foil firmly in place to the sides of the stone with ordinary masking tape. Finally, trim away all excess foil in your roll or square.

Now you are ready to commence the actual foiling process. Using the rounded edge of a wooden popcicle stick, and beginning at the center, press the thin foil delicately into the depressions underneath. Make sure that you do not press too hard, for foil has only limited elastic qualities before it begins to tear. As you continue, work the stick toward the edges along the niches, crevices, and contours. If you are working a carved scene along the border or at the top, be certain to depress all areas from all angles. In this way, you will be absolutely sure of extracting the entire portrait.

When you have completed the procedure outlined above, double-check all impressions in order to make sure that you have not inadvertently missed something. To do so, use a soft cloth or a wad of cotton to rub over the entire surface firmly one more time. Now, rub your hand across the surface and press ever so gently with your fingers, checking for any areas that may give slightly. The foil portrait should now resemble the tombstone in every detail, including intricate cracks and chips. If everything has been done correctly, you will have a completed artform ready to be removed.

To extract the foil from the stone, begin by carefully peeling the tape away from the secured edges. Next, bend the foil away from the wrapped turns in the marker, making certain that you do not tear it. Finally, with even more care than before, work the foil away from the face of the stone, beginning at the top and working your way toward the bottom. Presto -- you now have a foil etching which closely resembles a headstone from the past. In order to transport it safely home, wrap the foil art very loosely around an ordinary cardboard tube.

There are a number of finishing touches to choose from in completing your masterpiece. If you prefer to preserve it just the way it is, lay the foil face down on a flat surface with a number of newspaper layers underneath. Next, cover it with several coats of fiberglass resin, allowing each successive coat to harden before applying the next. In place of the fiberglass, sodium silicate (also known as waterglass) can be substituted.

When the foil is completely dry, turn it over once again and fill in the crevices and depressions with a light rubbing of liquid shoeblack, lino printing ink, or Indian ink. Next, when it dries once again, clean off the surplus polish or ink with fine steel wool. Finally, polish it delicately with a clean, soft cloth.

Another such procedure, which I refer to as foil flattening, can make a two-dimensional portrait appear to be three-dimensional in scope. To prepare your foil artwork for a step-by-step enhancement, simply take it home and pin it securely to a flat piece of cardboard.

The initial step is quite easy to carry out. Using black, or some other very dark spray paint, cover the entire foil with a light, solid coating. While doing so, make certain to cover all areas, including the deeply recessed spots. These same regions will hopefully be missed by the lighter colors that you will be using later. Furthermore, since lettering and other abrupt recessed places are normally in shadow on the real tombstone, the dark paint will give them the appearance of shadows in the finished product.

After allowing ample time for this dark base coat to dry, check to make certain that no unpainted foil remains visible. Now, using a spray paint which is quite a bit lighter (say blue or red), spray the surface in such a way that some portions are exposed to the paint while others are not. To accomplish this, hold the nozzle of the spray can at a sharp angle to the relief form, spraying horizontally from the right or left side along the surface instead of directly at it. Using this sharp "raking" angle, keep in mind that the striking contrast will be found in the next step. Before proceding further, allow ample drying time.

Now, from the opposite side (right or left), use a similar sharply raking angle to administer a much lighter color. I have found that, without question, white seems to work the best, though yellows, golds, or silvers are adequate substitutes.

When the paint is thoroughly dry, remove the pins and lay the foil out on a flat table with newspapers underneath. Next, pat and press the entire surface with the palm of your hand, working it into a flattened state once again. While doing so, it is absolutely essential that you do not smooth the wrinkles by stretching the foil. Instead, press straight down with a crushing movement; this will guarantee that you do not change the relative positioning of light and shadow. A smoothing and stretching motion would simply undo what you have worked so hard to do, thus causing surface distortion and ruining the three-dimensional illusion.

Finally, using an ordinary rolling pin, press the entire foil portrait so that it conforms with the table top. Soon, you will notice that the design is an exact copy of the gravestone surface. Furthermore, you will also see that every last detail has been faithfully preserved, transforming your work into a creation very similar to a photograph.

Using the above instructions, a professional foiler will soon learn that it doesn't matter how shallow the grave marker's relief is. Even the most weathered and difficult-to-transcribe tombstone portraits can be brought to life again with careful angling of the spray paint, and with the incorporation of strongly-contrasting color tones. In fact, even incisions that are only one-thirtieth of an inch in depth can be exaggerated to appear much deeper on the finished foil portrait. I found this to be true while I was working with a somewhat obscure epitaph in Cooke Memorial Park, Fairhaven, Massachusetts:

Sacred to the Memory of
John Cooke
Who was buried here in 1695
The last surviving male Pilgrim
Of those who came over in the
Mayflower
The first white settler of this town
And the pioneer in its religious
Moral and business life
A man
Of character and integrity
And the trusted agent for this
Part of the Commonwealth
Of the Old Colonial
Civil Government
Of Plymouth.

After attempting a simple pencil rubbing and failing miserably to capture the essence of the shallowly inscribed message, I decided to visit the local art supply store. Later, while employing a thin sheet of foil, the entire epitaph came out wonderfully.

Interestingly enough, a rather profound optical illusion may ocassionally occur while you are practicing your new-found art form. A completed foil will sometimes seem to undergo an unexplainable inversion, making it appear as if the light and shadow contrast has been reversed. I have seen similar results in photographs of the moon's surface on a particularly dark night - craters somehow seeming as if they were actually inflated bubbles, and high ridges collapsing deep into the surface. Then, almost magically, everything seems to snap back to normal.

Personally, I rather crave this optical illusion from my artwork, though you may not feel the same. If not, steps can be taken to control this visual trick, at least to some extent. If a particular marker's foiling persists in flip-flopping back and forth between appearances, place the art next to a lighted lamp within the confines of a somewhat darkened room so that shadows are cast in the correct direction. In doing so, the human eye is literally forced to see the image in the preferred way prior to painting.

If you wish to create a foil that goes beyond the simple reproductive stages, you might think about attempting to capture not only the portrait, but the feel and texture of the stone itself. To accomplish this, there are a few tricks of the trade that you can incorporate into your work.

First, the foil should be prepared prior to taking the tombstone's impression by crumpling it until it is wrinkled into a very fine and even texture. Now, smooth it out once again and roll it out as flat as humanly possible with your rolling pin. Notice how it has suddenly taken on a totally different texture. This is due to the mosiac of tiny folds you have created.

Aside from its altered texture, the aluminum foil will now be more flexible, and has become much more pliable. In fact, as you push it into the crevices and bumps of the stone, you will notice a large difference in the way it easily stretches to conformity. Furthermore, when you complete the process of spray painting, the end result will be a slightly rougher texture. Resembling an unpolished grave marker, which will have the coarse feeling of sandstone, your completed foil will now seem much more true to life.

Regardless of which method you choose to complete your foil creation, your artwork should not be glued flat to a mounting board or paper. If this is attempted, the finished product will tend to wrinkle and buckle within a matter of a few short hours. Technically, this marring effect is due to changing room temperatures which, in turn, causes the metal to expand and contract.

If, however, you do wish to mount the foil replica, use only a minimal amount of glue along the outermost edges of the design. Furthermore, at least one small edge area should be left open to "breathe," so that the air will not be trapped between the foil and the board. To avoid such problems, use a mat frame instead, gluing the design directly to the back of this "window." A stronger piece of cardboard or wood can then be implemented for backing. It should not, however, be adhered directly to the foil, but only the mat frame.

Unfortunately, despite all of your care in mounting and framing your creation, aluminum foil transfers will remain quite delicate. The slightest bit of pressure can cause the foil to crease and tear, or the sealer or paint to crack, chip, and flake. Furthermore, repairs are almost impossible to make. Obviously, if you are anything like me, you will want to simply get rid of the foil and keep the design. Precisely how this can be accomplished is described in detail in the following chapter.

Chapter 12

Tombstone Transfers

Phoebe S. Brashear
1834-1910
We have loved the stars too fondly
to be fearful of the night.
John S. Brashear
1840-1920.

Until the fifteenth century, people from Western Europe had employed a variety of materials on which to write. These included the soft, earthen clay often found within damp, eerie caverns; a substance made from the matted fiber of an ordinary marsh reed, known as papyrus; and surfaces devised from the stretching and drying of some animal skins, the result of which was referred to as vellum and parchment.

Still, for decades these substances remained less than ideal for their purpose, for they were either too fragile to work with or too costly to make. Hence, the search continued for a more available, inexpensive material. Little did Western Europeans know it at the time, though, but such an innovative technique had been used in faraway China for more than two hundred years. By drying out the watery pulp of regional vegetable fibers, these Oriental people had created a substance which would come to be called paper.

Western travelers into the Chinese region, such as the gem merchant Polo family of Venice, were destined to return home with samples of something Europeans had never laid eyes upon - printed money fashioned from paper. However, despite their widespread interest in the *product*, not one of these itinerant traders thought to bring the *process* of printing home with him. Yet, the idea did manage to take hold, and soon they developed their own revolutionary concept of transfer printing from stone.

To the modern-day tombstone sculpture and epitaph collector, transfer printing is a readily recognized art form. Carefully completed prints are replicas of the originals, right down to their clarity, texture, color tones, and shadows. And, unlike lithography and block printing, each is as unique as a fine photograph or exquisite portrait. Indeed, each possesses a character all its own.

Unlike the experiments conducted by Johann Gutenberg of Mainz, Germany, there is no "stamping" procedure involved with tombstone foil transfers. Instead, you will actually be removing the painted surface of an aluminum foil creation and placing it upon ordinary paper or some other material. In essence, no press is employed.

Though the step-by-step procedure which I am about to outline has been carried out by a great many early-day printers and modern-day artists, few have worked extensively with grave markers. Furthermore, I acquired these tried and true methods after hours of painstaking trial and error (most of which was "error").

It all started several summers ago as I traveled near the triangular inlet of Narragansett Bay in Providence, Rhode Island. While there, I leisurely shopped in a wide variety of arts and crafts outlets, which have become a mainstay of the commercialized East coast. I spent nearly a week spying breathtaking creations of elegant whaling ships, crusty sailors, and solemn lighthouses.

In one particular out-of-the-way beachfront shop, more noticable for its location than its art, I happened upon a painting of a magnificent seascape. Soft, sky blues and pinks intermixed with more radical sea greens, making it appear as real as a photograph. Yet right from the beginning I realized that this was no ordinary portrait. Moving closer to examine its strokes, I noticed that it had not been painted with a brush at all. Instead, it seemed to be stamped or printed directly onto the canvas. To my amazement, I spotted an almost identical copy of the same print hanging nearby. Perplexed, I asked the shopkeeper exactly how they had been created. It was then that I was first introduced to the interesting technique of aluminum foil transfer printing.

Not wanting to waste time delaying the application of my new-found knowledge, I set out to make a reproduction of one of the local tombstones. Unfamiliar with the various nooks and crannies of Providence, I first picked up a local map and purchased the necessary supplies from a nearby art retailer. Next, I drove to nearby Grace Church Cemetery, where I eventually found an ideal inscription to copy, which was dedicated to John Kerr:

I dreamt that buried in my fellow clay,
Close by a common beggar's side I lay;
Such a mean companion hurt my pride
And, like a corse of consequence, I cried,
Scoundrel begone; and henceforth touch me not,
More manners learn, and at a distance rot.
'Scoundrel' in still haughtier tones cried he,
Proud lump of earth, I scorn thy words and thee;
All here are equal, thou place now is mine,
This is my rotting place, and that is thine.

Though I methodically applied the steps that I had learned from the caretaker of the art shop, my ambitions were temporarily injured when the finished transfer came out looking like a blackened stove pipe. Although I did not understand at the time exactly what I had done wrong, by backtracking I believed that I had discovered the problem. Simply put, several essential steps that had been explained to me needed to be completed in a reorganized sequence. Whether it was my mistake in listening, or the shopkeep's mistake in explaining no longer mattered, for I was in the midst of making a true "discovery."

Satisfied that I knew now what I was doing, I tackled the exact same grave marker again; only this time I reversed the painting order. As I peeled the aluminum foil away from my construction paper (something you will learn more about very soon), I was shocked to see that I had made another "grave" error. All of the tombstone's lettering was printed in reverse order! I am happy to say, however, that these two poorly-conceived outcomes did not cause me to stop experimenting, for I have never been one to give up or give in. Eventually, the hit-and-miss steps I employed helped me to develop the following techniques.

Basically, depending on whether you're working with the carved artwork, the epitaph, or both, tombstone transfer methods will vary slightly from the same foundation concept. And since the basic step-by-step process is simply an extension of tombstone foiling (described in chapter 11), it will be much easier for you to comprehend if I begin with what I call reverse image transfer.

Prior to beginning your prototype project you should definitely go out shopping, taking the time to visit your local grocery, craft, drug, stationery, and/or art supply stores. There, you should purchase aluminum foil (thin varieties work best), masking tape, light and dark colored spray paints, large sheets of black or dark-colored construction paper, spray adhesive, and cotton balls. Furthermore, you should buy (if you don't already have

143

them) a sharp paper-cutter or scissors, a clean paint scraper, and tweezers. Now you are ready to begin.

Much like potato transfers, which many of us learned in elementary school classrooms all across America, reverse image printing reproduces a mirror print. To begin your project, choose a grave marker that exhibits a clean and easy-to-see sculpted image. I suggest a relatively small area of a particular stone, like a willow tree or a border design. For now, avoid working with the epitaphs you hope to capture, for these require a difference in the sequence of transferring steps, as well as some additional information. I will explain this technique a bit later.

Once again, prepare the stone in the usual way by excavating (if necessary), trimming away any bothersome tall grasses and branches, and giving the face of the marker a thorough cleaning. Next, make an aluminum foil impression of the artwork (*not* the epitaph), as was outlined in the last chapter. Now, remove it from the stone and transport it home, for you will definitely need a quiet, calm area in which to complete your work. As was the case with foiling, you are now ready to begin spray-painting the aluminum mold - only this time the procedure is a bit different than before. Instead of putting on the all-covering black base coat first, you will be completing this step *last.*

In carrying out the spray-painting process, begin by applying the lightest colors first. Remember, spray the depressed foil at a sharply raking angle from either the left or right of the inscription, and then allow ample time for it to dry. Next, from the opposite side (left or right, depending on your first light-colored spray), carefully apply some other light tone of paint. Once again, this is sprayed at a raking angle, and should be done with enough care that the opposing colors do not invade one another's surface territory. As before, allow plenty of time to dry. Now, repeat these two steps once again, making sure that all foil surfaces are bathed in light and slightly darker hues. Remember, you are attempting to create the painted illusion of light and shadow.

As you work, keep in mind that, when you have finished your transfer, only those colors that actually touch the foil will be seen. Furthermore, any paint that is sprayed over them now will in fact become mere background for the final masterpiece. So that you completely understand the importance of what you are doing, remember one more thing: it is this initial spraying of contrasting colors that will make all the difference in the world in your creation's final appearance.

Now that the foil is dry, flatten it carefully with the palm of your hand by pushing down on it firmly. Then, making sure not to stretch the foil, smooth it out with your rolling pin. Place newspapers underneath and cover the entire sheet with a final coat of the same color as the darkest one already applied. Though this particular step is not absolutely necessary, it will help to ensure that all foil surfaces have been completely covered.

Finally, you have reached a point in your work when the actual "transfer" of the portrait is carried out. First, lay a large sheet of the dark-colored construction paper, slightly larger than your flattened foil, over a thick layer of newspaper. Personally, I prefer black, since it is likely to conceal any mistakes that I might have made. Now, apply a thin coating of the spray adhesive to the construction paper by making an even, back-and-forth spraying motion across the surface. As you do so, overlap each preceding stroke by half, for it is all-important to adequately cover the entire sheet.

As the adhesive begins to dry, make sure to test it every few minutes by touching a small area with the tip of your finger. When it has gone beyond the wet stage, and reaches the point where it seems to be tacky (like the sticky side of masking tape), it is ready to accept the transfer.

Double-check your foiled design to see if it is, indeed, as flat as you can make it with your rolling pin. When you are satisfied that it is, carefully press it, paint side *down*, to the tacky side of the adhesive on the prepared construction paper. As you conduct this step, work from one edge of the foil to the opposite, smoothing and flattening it the best that you can as you continue to work. When this is done perfectly, the foil and the construction paper will seem like one sheet of material, with no bubbles or creases.

Next, using an ordinary cotton ball, rub the exposed side of the foil. After you have made it as smooth as possible, trim away the excess construction paper with a sharp paper-cutter or scissors. Now, repeat the rubbing process with a large, clean cotton ball or cotton cloth, bearing down on the foil with a good bit of muscle. If your cotton ball or cloth refuses to slide easily across the foil, try sprinkling on a small amount of talcum powder.

Despite all of your care, you still may see troublesome little air pockets, resembling tiny blisters, on the surface of the foil. If so, don't despair - I have found that releasing the pressure by poking minute pin holes in them seems to work just fine. In fact, this sort of "cheating" does not seem to harm the finished product in the least.

Now, using the flat side of your paint scraper, begin to "burnish" the flattened surface of the aluminum foil by stroking it in a squeegee-type fashion. In other words, with the metal edge of the scraper pointing at an angle away from you, draw the handle

145

back toward you (in an exact reverse action of scraping paint). Never, under any circumstances, should you *push* the sharp edge of the scraper across the foil. If you do, you will literally rip apart your foiled creation, and you will be forced to begin from scratch.

While burnishing the foil with the paint scraper, begin at the center and work your way out beyond the edges with single strokes. When the entire surface of the foil has been transformed into a glossy, smooth area, continue this process over and over again. Though it often takes a good deal of effort, time, and patience, you will eventually notice that the aluminum foil will begin to slightly separate from the construction paper. In the past, when I have been working the foil with my paint scraper, the two adhered materials normally begin to come apart at one of the corners. With the assistance of your handy tweezers, the foil can now be carefully pulled away from the construction paper.

Notice how the paint stays on the paper, stuck fast to the adhesive. If you have, indeed, done everything as you were supposed to, the design will be a mirror image of the original. Hence, now you understand why my original bout with epitaph transfers was a complete and utter failure; all the letters had come out in reverse.

In working with the tombstone's writings, you will need to tackle a type of transfer known as face-up printing. This process offers a creation that is not a mirror image, but one that is exactly identical to the painted foil in every detail. For this, in addition to the previously listed supplies, you will also need large pieces of white paper and a roll of transparent, self-adhesive plastic (contact paper seems to work the best).

In surveying the wide variety of epitaphs that you might find, I suggest that you choose one which is not only brief, but cut deep into the stone. Even though an epitaph is brief, it can be tremendously satisfying. Such is the case with an inscription I discovered in Crossroads Cemetery, Vineyard Haven, Massachusetts, over the grave of four-year-old Caroline Newcomb:

> She tasted of life's bitter Cup
> Refused to drink the Portion up
> But turned her little head aside
> Disgusted with the taste and died.

Or another example commemorating Triphena Shepard in Village Cemetery, Plainfield. Vermont:

> I would not live always.

If you do, indeed, choose an inscription that is brief and clear, there will be a far greater chance for success in transferring the design (since shallow engraving is much more difficult to work with). As you become more proficient in your hobby, however, you will be able to create concise copies of even the slightest incisions.

Once again, you should begin by making an aluminum foil impression of the stone's lettered inscription, as well as any chiseled artwork. Next, spray on a base coat of black paint, just as you did when making a simple foil design (the opposite of what we did in reverse image transfers). After this has dried, the lighter colors can be applied from two opposing raking angles. When the entire design is dry once again, flatten it first with the palm of your hand and then with the rolling pin. Now, position it so that it is facing up, with a slightly larger sheet of white paper underneath. Finally, smooth it out once again, and tack down the corners with masking tape, covering as little surface area with tape as possible. Place this part of your project off to the side for now.

Next, cut a piece of transparent contact paper from your roll, making it slightly larger than the white paper on which the foil is taped. Now for the tricky part: carefully remove the protective backing from the contact paper and tack the plastic, sticky side up, to a large piece of wood or cardboard. This, in fact, definitely sounds easier than it actually is, for contact paper can be a real problem to handle. If you have never worked with it before, there are some important pointers to remember. Otherwise, you may become adhered to the paper, much like a fly becomes entangled in fly paper.

The best approach to use in completing the above step without incident is to first gradually peel away the protective backing from the contact paper, exposing only one or two inches of adhesive plastic. Tack this uncovered edge to your wood or cardboard before peeling away most (but not all) of the remainder of the protective backing. As you do so, leave at least one or two inches along the opposite edge covered. Tack this side down to the wood or carboard prior to removing the remainder of the backing. You now have the most difficult part of the project well under control.

Now you are ready to make the actual face-up transfer. Like you did with the adhesive, place the painted aluminum foil creation against the contact paper, paint side down. To do so, begin with one edge of the foil and work your way toward the opposite edge, taking care to smooth out any large air pockets as you work. After you have completed this smoothing step, untack the contact paper from the cardboard or wood, and trim away the excess without cutting the foil. When you turn the design over, you will see a somewhat cloudy image through the plastic. You can now trim away a bit of the foil, including the masking tape.

At this stage of your work, the painted foil is not yet adhering tight enough to the contact paper. This is what causes the image to be extremely unclear. However, using a bit of muscle to rub a large, clean cotton ball or a piece of cotton cloth over the plastic will force the design to become much more distinct. Once again, pop any small air bubbles that may crop up. When you are satisfied that the image is as clear as it is going to get, rub it a while longer, then flip it back over.

Now, use your paint scraper in the same fashion as I described before, burnishing the foil from the center toward the outside edges. Once again, if you continue to stroke the foil the necessary length of time, it will slowly begin to separate from the contact paper. Peel it away carefully with your tweezers. The plastic print should then be smoothed out and glued to a large piece of dark construction paper. Finally, all you need do is mount your creation to a matting board or some other backing material.

If you find that you are not completely satisfied with this face-up transfer technique, you may choose to use something other than contact paper. In fact, I have discovered that acetate works just as well, if not better. Furthermore, you will not have to wrestle with the problem of adhering yourself to the paper.

To begin, return to your local art supply or craft store to purchase the sheets of clear plastic acetate. While shopping, remember that this product's thickness is measured in "points" (4 point, 7 point, etc.). In my opinion, the ideal thickness is 10 point acetate, which actually measures approximately 1/64 of an inch thick.

As usual, return to the cemetery and start by making an impression of the desired art and epitaph. Once again, spray it with a darker base coat, apply the opposing lighter colors, and allow enough time for the paint to dry. Now, as you did before, flatten the image with your hand and smooth it out with your rolling pin. Finally, positioning your design face up on a flat piece of white paper, carefully smooth it out and attach the corners to the paper with masking tape. You are now prepared to start the transfer process.

Employing a rather wide (three to four inch), flat, soft and tight-bristled paint brush, cover the entire surface of your painted foil with a very thin coat of undiluted polymer liquid gloss medium. This type of gloss is extremely important, since it never really becomes dry to the touch. Instead, when "dry," it actually remains somewhat tacky.

As you apply the gloss, do so in even, parallel strokes, making certain not to interrupt any particular stroke from one edge of the foil to the opposite edge. Soon after completing this step, and long before the gloss has become tacky-dry, carefully pull the design away from the paper to which it is taped. For the time being, set this safely off to the side.

Next, cut a piece of 10 point acetate to a size which is slightly larger than the foil. Prepare it in the same fashion that you did the foil, applying even, parallel strokes of polymer gloss to its exposed surface. After both the foil design and acetate have reached the stage of being tacky-dry, they are ready to be pressed together face to face. With the foil side of this "sandwich" facing upward, use a cotton ball or clean cotton cloth to smooth out the design. In carrying out this step, you will actually be forcing the two materials to reach their maximum adherence.

As previously described, use your paint scraper against the surface of the aluminum foil. Once again, as you continue to burnish the surface, the acetate and foil will begin to separate. The aluminum can then be peeled away, leaving the face up design on the acetate. If you eventually reach a point when you consider yourself somewhat of an expert at this technique, you may even try Plexiglass in place of the acetate plastic. It, above all other aforementioned materials, works the best if done carefully and correctly.

All that remains to be done now, regardless of which transfer method you used, is to place a protective covering over your transfer. As described in the chapter on rubbings, ordinary contact paper will help to protect it. However, I recommend that you have the construction paper framed and covered with glass. Certainly, in my opinion, this will make it look far more professional.

There you have it: a detailed how-to book on collecting tombstone art and epitaphs, including taking photographs, making rubbings, fashioning foil impressions, and conducting relief transfer projects. And, as you have clearly seen, for the avid hobbyist, whether he or she is an avid genealogical researcher or simply out searching for enjoyment, there are a number of ways to assemble a collection.

If I have helped you to gain some small bit of insight and knowledge concerning the various methods of collecting, then my effort has been well worthwhile. Furthermore, if I have spurred you toward the discovery and development of exciting new techniques, beyond what I have written, I would like to hear from you. In either case, knowledge shared is knowledge gained.

Bibilography

Adams, Ansel, *Natural-Light Photography*, Morgan & Morgan Inc., Hastings-on-Hudson, New York, 1952.

Alden, Timothy, *A Collection of American Epitaphs*, 5 volumes, New York, New York, 1814.

Andrews, William, *Curious Epitaphs*, London, England, 1899.

Arnold, Edmund C., *Ink On Paper*, Harper & Row, New York, New York, 1963.

Beable, W.H., *Epitaphs*, New York, New York, 1925.

Bowden, John, *The Epitaph-Writer: Consisting of Upwards of Six Hundred Original Epitaphs, Moral, Admonitory, Humorous, and Satirical: Numbered, Classed, and Arranged on a New Plan: Chiefly Designed for Those Who Write or Engrave Inscriptions on Tombstones*, Chester, London, England, 1791.

Bowdor, John, *Rubbings and Textures: A Graphic Technique*, Reinhold Book Corporation, New York, New York, 1968.

Coffin, Margaret M., *Death In Early America: The History and Folklore of Customs and Superstitions of Early Medicine, Funerals, Burials and Mourning*, Thomas Nelson, Inc., Nashville, Tennessee, 1976.

Cummings, J.W., *The Silver Stole, being a collection of One Hundred Texts of Scripture: and One Hundred Original Epitaphs, Suitable for The Grave of a Child*, New York, New York, 1859.

Duval, Francis Y. and Ivan B. Rigby, *Early American Gravestone Art in Photographs*, Dover Publications, Inc., New York, New York, 1978.

Eastman Kodak Company, *How To Make Good Pictures*, Amphoto, New York, New York, 1967.

Forbes, Harriette Merrifield, *Gravestones of Early New England*, Da Capo Press, New York, New York, 1967.

Gillon, Edmund Vincent, Jr., *Early New England Gravestone Rubbings*, Dover Publications, Inc., New York, New York, 1966.

Hill, Douglas, *Magic and Superstition*, Hamlyn Publishing Group Ltd., London, England, 1968.

Hirsch, S. Carl, *Printing From A Stone: A Story of Lithography*, The Viking Press, New York, New York, 1967.

Howe, Walter Henry, *Here Lies*, New York, New York, 1901.

Jones, Mary Ellen, "Photographing Tombstones: Equipment and Techniques," American Association for State and Local History, *History News*, February, 1977.

Ludwig, Allan L., *Graven Images*, Wesleyan University Press, Middletown, Connecticut, 1966.

Richings, Benjamin, *Voices From the Tombs*, London, England, 1858.

Rogers, Frances, *Painted Rock To Printed Page*, J. B. Lippincott, Co., Philadelphia, Pennsylvania, 1960.

Simon, Irving B., *The Story of Printing*, Harvey House, Irvington-On-Hudson, New York, 1964.

Skinner, Michael Kingsley, *How To Make Rubbings*, Van Nostrand Reinhold Company, New York, New York, 1972.

Stevens, Harold, *Relief and Design Transfer*, Davis Publications, Inc., New York, New York, 1974.

Strangstad, Lynette, *A Gravevard Preservation Primer*, The American Association for State and Local History, Nashville, Tennesee, 1988.

Wallis, Charles L., *Stories On Stone*, Oxford University Press, New York, New York, 1954.

INDEX

This index references the general subject matter pertaining to tombstones to be found in this book.